CONTESTED
SITES IN
EDUCATION

CRITICAL EDUCATION & ETHICS

Barry Kanpol
General Editor

Vol. 6

The Critical Education and Ethics series is part of the Peter Lang Education list.
Every volume is peer reviewed and meets
the highest quality standards for content and production.

PETER LANG
New York • Bern • Frankfurt • Berlin
Brussels • Vienna • Oxford • Warsaw

CONTESTED SITES IN EDUCATION

The Quest for the Public Intellectual,
Identity and Service

Edited by **KAREN RAGOONADEN**

PETER LANG
New York • Bern • Frankfurt • Berlin
Brussels • Vienna • Oxford • Warsaw

Library of Congress Cataloging-in-Publication Data

Contested sites in education: the quest for the public intellectual, identity and service /
edited by Karen Ragoonaden.
pages cm. — (Critical education and ethics; vol. 6)
Includes bibliographical references and index.
1. College teachers—Professional ethics. 2. College teachers—Professional relationships.
3. Educational leadership—Moral and ethical aspects.
4. Education, Higher—Aims and objectives.
I. Ragoonaden, Karen, editor of compilation.
LB1779.C53   174.9378—dc23   2014033088
ISBN 978-1-4331-2507-2 (hardcover)
ISBN 978-1-4331-2506-5 (paperback)
ISBN 978-1-4539-1435-9 (e-book)
ISSN 2166-1359

Bibliographic information published by **Die Deutsche Nationalbibliothek**.
Die Deutsche Nationalbibliothek lists this publication in the "Deutsche
Nationalbibliografie"; detailed bibliographic data are available
on the Internet at http://dnb.d-nb.de/.

The paper in this book meets the guidelines for permanence and durability
of the Committee on Production Guidelines for Book Longevity
of the Council of Library Resources.

© 2015 Peter Lang Publishing, Inc., New York
29 Broadway, 18th floor, New York, NY 10006
www.peterlang.com

Printed in the United States of America

To all those
Who truly see the similarities in the differences

Table of Contents

Introduction

Ethical Teacher Dilemmas
in a Neoliberal Age

KAREN RAGOONADEN

Emerging from the confines of an academic institution in transition from a college to a university, this book offers provocative insights into the impact of change on the sense of agency and the ensuing consequences on the personal and professional identities of seven academics at various stages of their career. Recognizing the serious debate surrounding the raison d'être of higher education (Christensen & Eyring, 2011; Emberley, 1996), this volume explores how faculty members wrestled with the inherent tension of the corporatization of the university ensconced in research intensive mandates and the challenge of fulfilling their formative mission: to develop intellectual and cultural resources to prepare themselves and their students for lives of significance and responsibility (Sullivan & Rosin, 2008). As members of a Faculty of Education, the authors were responsible for preparing educators for the profession of teaching and accountable to the accreditation standards established by the governing bodies of education. Consequently as scholar practitioners, their research agenda was often field based and applied, and as public intellectuals they strove to influence change and direction in policy and practice in the profession. Yet, despite their professional and ethical commitments to their students and to education, the pervasive neo-liberal agenda with its emphasis on productivity and accountability for research output significantly affected the culture and nature of work of academics, particularly those who have not yet attained the security and perceived increased academic freedom that comes with tenure.

With heightened attention to the performance measures that merit tenure and promotion and the deep-rooted anxiety and insecurity this creates regarding what counts as meritorious work, these academics strove to make a difference in society and in schooling by engaging in projects that befit society as a whole. Cognizant of higher education's public purpose and service in a democratic society, these narrative inquiries coupled with research-based initiatives encourage a reassessment of presumptions and assumptions about the nature and value of an academic's professional and scholastic engagement. These profiles alternately present images of success and failure encountered by sessional, tenure-track, and tenured colleagues as they navigate the detritus left by market-driven forces. Within this context, university educators are positioned as committed agents of change, advocating for public policies and practices that benefit the students they serve, their colleagues, and the communities they live in to build a more just, inclusive, democratic community. Higher education, particularly Faculties of Education, can be forums where university educators practice institutional, cultural, and political innovations by teaching students to deconstruct the reproduction of meanings of individual success, competitiveness, egotistic desires, sexism, and racism that emerge out of dominant ideology and worldviews. By promoting transformative paradigms in Faculties of Education, the narrative inquiries and research initiatives offer the possibility to examine the inherent and inherited social constructs of a professional faculty caught in the flux of tradition, modernity, postmodernity, alternate views of higher education, engagement, and commitment.

Culminating in critical reflections about teaching, research, and service, the aim of this chronicle is to empower educators as they progress toward intellectual autonomy, able to emancipate themselves from the embedded educational status quo and the looming shackles of performativity. By sharing their stories, these pedagogues bring a heightened awareness to the struggle to maintain academic freedom and the right to pursue research that is in the public interest and to contribute new knowledge to the profession. From these records, we come to understand how the demands for performativity reflected in the quest for high teaching scores, funded research, and peer-reviewed publications have a profound impact on the kinds of research worth doing, turning academics away from their mission as public intellectuals and transformative scholars into instrumental cogs in the corporate machine of a research-intensive institution. In the pursuit of tenure and promotion, these colleagues share their reluctance to be innovative, to engage in research on the margins, and to challenge the authority of the dominant norms of what constitutes being a successful academic.

Written with courage and conviction, the following chapters offer brief glimpses into the lived experiences of early-career, mid-career, and senior scholars. In keeping with their engaged and committed approach to teaching and learning, the authors deconstruct patterns of alienation, oppression, and discrimination experienced in professional contexts. They decry the inherent competition, the inherited focus on individualism, and the intrinsic self-promotion of the contemporary professor of education. These educators emphasize that practice and praxis including curriculum must be reconceptualized as a platform for active negotiation, for knowledge mobilization, and for knowledge construction. To do so, teacher educators must shoulder the responsibility for collegial governance by contesting the measures used to determine meritorious academic work. Furthermore, these academics need to situate the moral imperative of their work as teacher educators by recognizing their impact factor, particularly as scholar-practitioners and public intellectuals. Reminiscent of Kanpol's (2010) call for reform in higher education infused with a moral imperative, the following paragraphs offer a brief overview of the main tenets of the authors' work.

In "Setting the Path Toward Emancipatory Practices: Professor of Teaching," Karen Ragoonaden reflects on the transformative process of reconceptualizing the pathway to a tenured academic position to include the traditional academic research stream as well as a valued teaching stream. She shares her experiences of being one of the first faculty members in the university to seek tenure in the newly conceived Professor of Teaching stream. Hired into an institution that was formerly a university college (with a focus on teaching) in the process of becoming a research university, Ragoonaden found that this organization did not have the benefit of established processes, resources, and parameters for conceptualizing and supporting young academics to develop robust programs of research. The tenure clock ticking, this assistant professor made the prudent decision to choose the newly developed Professor of Teaching stream. The novel rank reflected the commitment of the university to recognize the importance of teaching, equating it with research. Those seeking tenure in this stream were expected to provide educational leadership and curriculum innovation in the sphere of higher education. Her story reflects the challenges of seeking tenure in a stream that existed in policy, but which had not yet been tested in practice. As the pioneer for this stream, she encountered challenges by human resources, senior administration, and her tenured colleagues as to what constitutes the meritorious work of this stream, how it should be supported and measured, and what it means to be a Professor of Teaching in an institution striving to be research intensive. Her story reflects her experience of the disintegration of her personal and professional identity, and experiences of otherness and marginalization in her pursuit of being a scholar practitioner within the emergent Professor of Teaching stream.

"Dwelling Artfully in the Academy: Walking on Precarious Ground" reconstructs and reflects on significant "stop moments" (Appelbaum, 1995) in the life of an emerging scholar. In a narrative intensely personal and provocative, Pamela Richardson explores the disconnect that exists between the practice of art and common forms of earning a living. Recognizing that there are categories of human enterprise that are not well organized or supported by market forces, she observes her work as a teacher educator and educational researcher wither under the exchange values and analytics of the marketplace. Acknowledging that artistic engagement is not a valued pathway through the academy, she seeks, in the words of Hyde (1979/2007), "nonmarket ways to organize" her relationship to her scholarship, students, and colleagues as the fundament for academic life. Wishing for a scholarship of mindful and artful relations as an alternative, she battles against those forces that would break down imaginative action and thought in the name of pseudo-educational discourses based in marketplace rationales. Through her evocative poetry, she seeks to understand what it means to dwell artfully as a researcher and practitioner in a twenty-first-century Faculty of Education.

"Ideology, Performativity, and the University" recognizes the chaotic impact of neoliberalism and accountability in higher education. Catherine Broom acknowledges that this agency of change is shaping the culture of academia and the practices of academics. Citing Ball (2006), she identifies performativity as mechanisms of control manifested in myriad ways through various modes of regulation. In higher education, specific examples of performativity include the ranking of universities and the stringent, accountability-based evaluation of professors for tenure. Lyotard (Ball, 2002) argues this is a system of "terror" that employs judgments, comparisons, and displays as means of control, attrition, and change. Since performativity controls behavior, the performances of individual subjects of organization serve as a measure of productivity or output. Through archival research relating to the culture and responsibilities of university professors, Broom elaborates on current administrative changes influencing the work of academics in relation to the neoliberalism agenda and performativity. She includes the results of a survey of a small sample of Canadian academics regarding their perspectives on how performativity has influenced their work. Concluding with a series of recommendations focusing on how to manage performativity, this inquiry explores how ideology and contemporary social and economic conditions affect personal and professional academic identity in twenty-first-century Faculties of Education.

In "Living and Working in a Global Space: Liminality Within an Academic Life," Susan Crichton, an established educator who joined the academy at age 50, surveys her experiences in making her transition into the academy to pursue meaningful work. Crichton acknowledges she naively took the stance that meaningful, good work – that which makes a difference to practitioners in the field (Räsänen, 2008; Shulman, 2005) – would lead to merit, promotion, and tenure. She illustrates with unequivocal honesty the discordance between personally and professionally "worthy" projects and those anointed by the academy as research-worthy in terms of merit and tenure. Informed by educators such as Daniel (2010), she argues academics can democratically participate in educational reform that could lead to the nurturing of human capabilities that afford the freedom to lead worthwhile lives

(Thomas & Brown, 2011; Trilling & Fadel, 2009), and these endeavors should not merely train individuals to become the human capital required for economic production (Daniel, 2010, p. 6). This chapter positions "worthy" scholarship and academic work within challenging contexts, recognizing the importance of researching "with" rather than "about" colleagues in those settings. Through examining her experiences of liminality in living and working globally, she explores being an outsider in a global setting as well as becoming an outsider in her local context. Her development of an ever-expanding worldview and time away from home campus and community leaves her at this portal between both worlds, not really a full member of either.

In "Performativity in the Academy: Negotiating Ambition, Desire, and the Demands of Femininity," Lynn Bosetti and Sabre Cherkowski share the narratives of five academic women at various stages in their careers to address the demands of their personal lives and the normative scripts of being successful academics. They argue that professional faculties are regulated by an inherited social structure and organizational culture that influences their professional identity. They reside in this double entanglement of addressing the demand of performativity in their academic work, and the impact on addressing the expectations for their role and responsibilities in their personal lives. They lament the desire for an undivided life where they experience harmony in their professional and personal identity.

Using Bradotti's (1994) feminist genealogy, these researchers documented narratives provided by female academics detailing the trials and tribulations of scholarly pursuits. The results of their study indicate that the omniscient culture of professional faculties is particularly problematic for academic women. Positioned between the demands of femininity and those of intellectual life, female academics often have to compartmentalize and counterbalance each of their distinct identities as scholar, wife, and mother. This narrative provides a space where academic women can join together to reflect on and challenge the social interpretations of personal and professional identities by sharing stories of struggle, resistance, surrender, and, finally, compromise.

In "On the Educational Value of Philosophical Ethics: A Reflection on the Problem of 'Relevance' in Teacher Education," Christopher Martin analyzes the extent to which philosophical ethics can articulate its educational value for teacher candidates. Specifically, how can philosophers of education conceptualize, and account for, their ethical work with teachers? By presenting an overview of philosophical ethics in education, the author advances the argument that teachers should be initiated into understanding moral inquiry as an intellectual tradition. Therefore, the dialectic presented is not how philosophy can "be relevant" in the strictly economic sense but how it ought to identify and address such problems that have consequence for "somebody, somehow, somewhere, and someone." By setting out an agenda for action and by expanding on the normative criteria of "significance," the chapter discusses the question of the socioeconomic feasibility of democratic aims of education under conditions of competitive global capitalism.

Sabre Cherkowski's "Developing Mindful Teacher Leader Identities in Higher Education" explores the challenges and implications for fostering and cultivating teacher leadership as a moral agenda for authentic learning in higher education. In particular, she examines how teacher leaders develop a sense of identity around what it means to become a teacher leader and what it means to live out this role in professional contexts. As the demand for teacher leadership development increases, she ponders the following questions: What is the university teacher preparation program's role in developing teacher leaders? How might we conceive of teacher leadership as a habit of mind, or as a way of engaging in ways of knowing that cultivate a sense of practical wisdom? Could this discerning, deliberate, informed, and thoughtful way of thinking perhaps be construed as mindful teacher leadership? Specifically, this chapter explores these questions and examines the opportunities and challenges for university teacher education programs to conceptualize and develop mindful teacher identities in education.

The last chapter of this text is conceptualized as a reflective, post-formal response from a dean of a Faculty of Education. From an educational point of view, of particular interest are the comments regarding the imposter syndrome. Lynn Bosetti argues that this state of mind is indicative of the academic (human) condition, particularly relevant for those academics caught in the liminal space of sessional, tenure-track, and tenured work as well as college instructors navigating their status and success with the expectations of being a university professor. She warns against the cult of busyness and perpetuating the culture of constantly producing without discernment regarding what projects are worth producing. She acknowledges the tendency for academic work to engulf identity, providing thin boundaries between personal and professional lives. She reminds faculty that in the spirit of collegial governance, university professors have the opportunity to challenge the dominant culture and contest the demand of performativity by co-creating shared values of what constitutes good and worthwhile work in a faculty of education, and supporting work-life balance.

These testimonies emanating from university colleagues emphasize the complexity of teaching, research, and service in higher education. Their voices reflect the nexus of Kanpol's (1999) epistemology, "To what end do we do what we do?" representing the inherent contradictions in the quest for a professional and public identity. These transformative scholar practitioners attest to the importance of unifying the voices of like-minded colleagues in teacher education, and of searching for the similarities within differences to develop cohesive faculty-wide epistemologies focusing on libratory practices infused with the possibility and the vision of an agency of change.

In this age of productivity and performativity, as we navigate our way through the mass reconceptualization of faculties of education, university educators find themselves in what Bhabha (1994) terms a Third Space: a liminal, transitory reality caught between capitalistic market-driven outcomes and the Deweyian quest for public intellectualism steeped in moral and ethical behaviours. Yet, we understand that we do not stand alone.

Emerging from the complexity and the chaos of a university in transition, the contributing authors of this volume offer educators praxis-oriented, hope-infused, contemplative approaches to conceiving, developing teaching, research, and public service paradigms. Rising above the fray of the neoliberal agenda, the focus is to prepare mindful educators who thoroughly understand, consciously apply, and intentionally use democracy, self-knowledge, cultural knowledge, habits of mind, reflective practice, and advocacy in their professional and personal lives (Ball & Tyson, 2011).

CHAPTER ONE

Setting the Path Toward Emancipatory Practices

Professor of Teaching

KAREN RAGOONADEN

Arising from the contested site of a new university campus, this chapter reflects on the transformative process of reconceptualizing and rebuilding a professional and academic stream in a twenty-first-century Faculty of Education. In particular, the discussion will reflect the impact of this agency of change on one tenure-track faculty member who was hired into a new research-intense university at a time when the campus did not possess resources and parameters for conceptualizing, supporting, and developing research. To maximize her capital, this assistant professor sought tenure in an innovative new stream introduced to her campus, Professor of Teaching. The novel rank reflected the commitment of the university to provide educational leadership, outstanding teaching, and curriculum innovation to higher education. However, despite the fact that outstanding achievement was required in these areas, guidelines for promotion to Professor were not directive and exhaustive but more so suggestive and situated in place-based environments. Within the context of a market-driven and policy-laden postsecondary institution, this was problematic. Since evidence supporting promotion to full professor is dependent on the discipline and the Faculty, myriad interpretations of what exactly constituted a Professor of Teaching emerged. Chaos, blunders, and misunderstandings ensued. Based on the ambiguity of these policies, of singular interest is the discussion surrounding the experiences of *otherness and marginalization* that arose as this scholar practitioner focused on her work as a teacher educator and a researcher in an emergent rank in a nascent university.

Confronted with the inherent complexities and indistinctness of this new rank, this author pondered: *What is my scholarly role as a Professor of Teaching in a Faculty of Education? How does this role affect personal, professional, and academic integrity and identity?* Recognizing the transformative nature of higher education as an important gateway to desirable employment, this narrative examines how a teacher educator conceptualizes the practical application of the academy's educational formative mission: to develop intellectual and cultural resources to prepare students for lives of significance and responsibility (Sullivan & Rosin, 2008).

Along with this examination, an ancillary contentious issue in higher education, the highly competitive, self-positioning tenure and promotion process, will serve as a secondary thematic for further discussion.

TENURE AND PROMOTION

Taking its roots in European universities during the Middle Ages, the purpose of tenure was to protect a scholarly culture where teaching and writing could proceed without reprisals from the reigning, dominant powers. However, now the reality of tenure and promotion is fraught with strife: faculty focusing on research while neglecting teaching and service; questions surrounding the objectivity of research; productive faculty straining under the combined pressures of research, teaching, and service; tenured faculty abandoning early scholarly ambitions and making no contributions to scholarship and mentorship of junior colleagues; and contentious relationships with corporate partners (Côté & Allahar, 2007; Emberley, 1996). Due to the existing turmoil in the university culture, there exists a sense that higher education institutions are no longer meeting the demands of contemporary society and are not preparing students with background, skills, and flexibility to become leaders in the global knowledge economy.

Critical educational theorists have long argued that democracy provides a forum to explore the imperatives of living in a diversified society by giving voice to the struggle of various groups to challenge personal and institutional forms of oppression, alienation, and subordination related to race, class, and gender (Ball & Tyson, 2011; Giroux, 1992; Kanpol, 1999; Kanpol & McLaren, 1995; Kincheloe, 2005; Kozol, 1991; Shor,1992). Despite this rhetoric, universities, fueled by neoliberal, market logic-led driven mandates, are increasingly moving away from the founding democratic principles espoused by educational philosophers like Dewey (1897, 1902, 1916, 1927) to embrace corporate ideologies mired in commerce, competition, standardization, and individualism.

Within this context, this chronicle posits that university educators, as committed agents of change, should be advocating for practices that benefit society as well as emergent transformative scholarly cultures in academia to build just, inclusive, democratic communities. As an evolving rank, the Professor of Teaching validates and acknowledges the importance of the scholarship of teaching and learning at a micro-level in Faculties of Education, and on a macro-level, campuswide across the university. Historically, Faculties of Education have suffered the brunt of marginalization and focused biases relating to the perceived lesser quality of research such as poor conceptualizations and definitional problems done in professional contexts (Pajares, 1992). Since criteria related to promotion in the Professor of Teaching stream are adaptable and amenable to diverse interdisciplinary contexts, progress in this rank has the potential to provide consistency and adherence in teaching and research in Faculties of Education, acknowledging the primary pedagogical mandate of universities. Higher education, particularly Faculties of Education, can be forums where university educators practice institutional, cultural, political, intellectual, and pedagogical innovations by modelling paradigms that deconstruct the reproduction of meanings of individual success, competitiveness, egotistic desires, sexism, and racism that emerge out of normative ideology and worldviews. The aim of this critical reflection is to empower scholar practitioners progressing toward intellectual autonomy and emancipation from the traditional university status quo by becoming active participants, eager and competent to engage in processes of social transformation. On the part of the modern, contemporary professor of teaching, this requires evidence of outstanding teaching, critically creative consciousness, curricular innovation, and distinction in educational leadership at the local, national, and international levels.

In keeping with the above and in particular with Peters, Alter & Schwartzbach's (2010) normative positions about the roles and contributions of academic professionals, the author embarked on a research project exploring the multiple civic and public dimensions of scholarly work through a self-study of teacher and teacher education practices (S-STEP). Specifically, this research reflects on the impact of scholarly and cultural marginalizations and otherness observed in urban schools and mirrored in the university educator's experience, as she progressed through the new rank of Professor of Teaching in a Faculty of Education. It is within this context that an investigation of the influences that shape a teacher educator's role and practice were examined. To infuse objectivity into the study, critical pedagogy provided the means and the methods to facilitate reflection on inequalities and social injustices in educational settings as well as the scholar-practitioner's earned and unearned privilege in society. Through a critical pedagogy framework using S-STEP, this teacher educator reflected on cultural knowledge, self-knowledge, habits of mind, and reflective communities of practice as well as their impact on the complexity of practice. As indicated in the literature, the creation of these critically reflective types of learning can pave the way for an agency of change by contributing to the development of effective teaching practices in diverse and inclusive contexts (Egbo, 2009; Gay, 2003; Haberman & Post, 1992; Ladson-Billings, 2006; Parhar & Sensoy, 2011; Villegas & Lucas, 2002).

INCLUSIVE EDUCATIONAL PRACTICES

In the twenty-first century, the adoption of inclusive educational practices that validate the cultural, linguistic, and differential learning styles of underrepresented and minority groups have become a necessity. However, research shows that some educators are reluctant to adopt progressive, transformative approaches. Due to this resistance in the field and in teacher education programs, reproduction of social inequalities based on socioeconomic class-based differences are still being legitimized in educational institutions (Grant & Gibson, 2011).

Studies in diversity education also indicate that teachers' beliefs and traditions can either reinforce race, class, and gender inequities or, depending on best practice, validate multiple understandings and ways of being (Ball & Tyson, 2011). Emerging as a global trend, pluralistic societies can position teacher educators as leaders whose aim is to provide opportunities for all school students to access social and cultural capital, a necessary condition for developing socioeconomic mobility.

SELF-STUDY

The methodology of self-study is a recognized research and practice employed by educators to improve practice and student learning (Laboskey, 2007; Pinnegar, 1998). Laboskey (2007) identifies the following characteristics of self-study: self-initiated, focused, improvement-aimed, interactive, multiple mainly qualitative methods. Like critical pedagogy, Self-Study of Teachers and Teacher Education Practices (S-STEP) is founded on postmodern and feminist epistemology relating to emancipation through knowledge and the "political commitment to oppressed groups" (Samaras, Hicks, & Garvey Berger, 2007, p. 908). Accordingly, its aim is to "provoke, challenge, and illuminate rather than conform and settle" (Laboskey, 2007, p. 818). The focus of self-study examines the intersection of theory and practice, research and pedagogy, the self and the other with the intent to discover the hidden personal narratives about higher education, school, and schooling and its impact on the way teachers teach students. In this respect, an examination of the self juxtaposed with an examination of one's professional environment becomes tantamount to understanding and accepting difference and otherness in pedagogical contexts (Heilman, 2003).

CRITICAL PEDAGOGY

The conscious act of applying critical theory to an educational context is referred to as critical pedagogy (Kanpol, 1999; Kanpol & McLaren, 1995). Taking its roots in Western Marxist philosophy and postmodern ideals of emancipation and libratory approaches to teaching and learning, critical pedagogy provides a forum in which teacher candidates reflect on, identify, and question dominant ideology. By recognizing that public institutions covet the reproduction of the economic, political, social, and cultural mores of a dominant worldview, educators can develop awareness of the lack of opportunities available to those *other*, *hidden* voices that populate their classrooms. Grant and Gibson (2011) reviewed studies that demonstrate how teachers' class, race, and gender affected their worldviews, values, and educational practices. These differences were representative of distinctive socioeconomic and cultural stratifications that either ensured or negated life chances of underrepresented populations. Research also acknowledges that despite emancipatory praxis-oriented approaches, most teacher educators still adhere to beliefs that strengthen institutionalized racism, white privilege, and normative narratives of identity (Egbo, 2005, 2009; Gay, 2003; Haberman & Post, 1992; Ladson-Billings, 2006; Parhar & Sensoy, 2011; Villegas & Lucas, 2002). To further complicate matters within the North American educational context, it is recognized that teachers have had little preparation for working in culturally diverse classrooms and even less exposure to concepts relating to critical pedagogy and critical multiculturalism (Apple, 2004; Nieto, 2004; Shariff, 2008; Villegas & Lucas, 2002). All teachers and teacher educators can be better prepared for teaching by bridging the gap between demographics, experiences, and cultural values (Ball, 2009; Bascia, 1996; Casey, 1993; Henry, 1995; Mogadime, 2004; Nieto, 2004).

As stated, critical theory literature examines the multiple social relationships of race, class, and gender in schools and in society (Giroux, 1983; Kanpol, 1999; Kanpol & McLaren, 1995; Shor, 1992). This conceptualization provides a lens through which traditional educational practices based on the technocratic limitations of class size, space, official curriculum, political agendas, linear teaching, and learning can be renegotiated.

RECONCEPTUALIZING TEACHER EDUCATION: A PERSONAL PERSPECTIVE

As I progressed through the rank of Professor of Teaching, attaining the much-heralded tenure, I sought to make a difference in my practice and in the experiences of my mostly white, female, middle-class students. However, before I embarked on this journey, in my own professional life, as an assistant professor, subtle signs of change, particularly demotion, were becoming present. I was granted tenure not as Associate Professor but as a Senior Instructor. Funding relating to conference presentations was denied, as was participation in important departmental committees such as Tenure and Promotion. When I questioned and interrogated these policies, I was met with condescension and indifference. Senior administrators imperceptibly inferred that faculty in the Professor of Teaching did not possess the necessary qualifications to discuss or to disseminate new knowledge relating to the scholarship of teaching and learning or to make grounded, objective judgments relating to colleagues' research dossiers in the tenure and promotion process. Bolstered by indignation, I embarked on a torturous circuit leading to Human Resources, the Faculty Association, and finally back to the Faculty of Education. This was to no avail. Repeatedly, I was met with a scalding rhetoric about my place and position. Through the steady devaluation of my academic identity, the attempt to muzzle my questions, and the abrupt dismissal of my concerns, I recognized the deskilling permeating my academic environment. In a concept taken from nineteenth-century industry, Kincheloe (2005) explains how the phenomenon of deskilling the industrialized worker and the teacher are similar. A teaching practice can be reduced to an automated, technocratic, bland output mandated by a set curriculum. According to interpretations made by senior administration, a Professor of Teaching focused solely on teaching, keeping abreast of current developments and establishing a nationwide reputation. However, a critical analysis of praxis resulting in research was neither encouraged nor funded. In this instance, the lack of critical consciousness promoted by senior administration was impeding the progression of creative, critically infused innovative pedagogy. Reflective teaching became secondary since the expectation was that outcome-based subject and content area were being transmitted to students. One of the aims of critical pedagogy is to empower the voices of educators who through systematic bureaucratic impositions have lost their ability to objectively assess information and tasks prescribed by the pedagogical hierarchy. However, in the case of this new rank, it seemed that a deskilling process was being initiated by the university administration aimed squarely at teaching faculty.

University policy, led by a vanguard of an older generation schooled in Eurocentric conceptions of scholarly activity, considered Professor of Teaching faculty to be ancillary. Based on anecdotal evidence, these career administrators seemed oblivious to their lack of knowledge concerning academic and educational diversity. I recognized the monumental importance of reconceptualizing tenure and promotion in North America, dare I say, reconceptualizing teacher education programs in North America. Choosing my battles with care, I came to realize and reflect on existing educational inequities in society.

Considering the rapidly growing number of aboriginal students and children of color as well as the low numbers of minority teachers and administrators in public schools, this was a tenet well worth discussing in both policy and practice spheres. In keeping with the problematization present in teacher education programs, Barrón (2008) speaks to the cognitive dissonance apparent in discourses when discussing race, power, and privilege. She has observed the niggling discomfort of teacher candidates struggling with notions of cultural identity. Sleeter (2001) notes that many white teachers avoid discussing issues of race, minimize the extent and impact of racial discrimination, and refuse to discuss race openly, emphasizing *the myth of racelessness* (Brown, 2005). This destabilizing of beliefs and the disruption of uncontested privilege could provide important scaffolding in an examination of traditional ideological conceptions of scholarly performativity and of student learning and behavior.

It is important that scholar practitioners at universities be required to critique all aspects of their work through conference presentations, peer-review, and research. This type of critical consciousness involves interrogating the multiple, complex interpretations of pedagogy while interrupting mainstream ideological discourses that reinforce the reproduction of normative curricular and assessment practices. Educators who demonstrate critical consciousness can then begin to question their own positions, assumptions, and beliefs about themselves and others, thus leading the way toward transformative praxis affecting antiquated university policy. However, in the Professor of Teaching stream this access to criticality was being denied due to institutional policies disallowing funding for travel and participation on tenure and promotion committees. In effect, a deskilling of the professoriate was taking place.

TRANSFORMATIVE PRAXIS

Bartolomé (2004, 2008), a university educator, has studied and provided a model for the implementation of critical consciousness. She employs critical pedagogy in her work to help teacher candidates develop ideological clarity. She concludes that practice and research in teacher education must include implicit study of ideology in coursework, field placement, and service-learning opportunities. Consequently, scaffolding through conceptual frameworks that can help researchers investigate racism or classicism, specific guidelines for carrying out inquiry, teacher modeling of shared narrative experiences, and providing models and support for practice in critical reflection is a necessary step toward developing critical consciousness. In keeping with Bartolomé's stance, developing critical consciousness in a methodic and calculated manner in Faculties of Education seems to be necessary to counter hegemonic, traditional stances in higher education. In theory, the educational leadership and curricular innovation espoused by the Professor of Teaching stream should promote analytical reflection, not a deskilling of critical skills.

In keeping with Bartolomé's (2004, 2008) and Brown's (2005) focus on developing criticality in a progressive scaffolding, self-study and self-knowledge become important pieces in transforming pedagogy and practice. In higher education, researchers acknowledge that when critical reflection is missing from teacher education programs, teacher candidates adopt a technocratic rational approach in the classroom unaware of the impact of the pedagogical and moral consequences of their actions. By providing solid parameters for reconstructing significant life events and analyzing these circumstances on an ongoing basis, educators should be able to embark on the path of developing professional identity and integrity by exploring pathways between knowledge and practice particularly in educational contexts.

CULTURAL KNOWLEDGE AND SELF-KNOWLEDGE

As I progressed through my academic career in the Professor of Teaching stream, I continued my teaching, place-based research and service focusing on culturally relevant education in minority contexts. Through my writing, I came to understand the multilayered parallels that existed between my academic work and my career progression. By choosing to be tenured into the Professor of Teaching rank, I had been positioned into a minority, marginalized career path. Having chosen an academic path focusing on teaching, I had, inadvertently, ventured into a subordinate stream where I was gradually being deskilled and pulled away from my critical consciousness and research initiatives. Coupled with a substantial teaching load, access to the cultural capital and habitus of university life was withdrawn: internal funding and participation in tenure and promotion committees. I was being deskilled. The act of reskilling deskilled teachers begins with the development of critical awareness and actions that foster change and progress. In higher education, this critical awareness is developed through local, national, and international conference presentations, peer-review, research, and publications. By negating opportunities for funding and participation on important committees, the dominant, conservative university culture was in effect, removing any potential or ability for promotion. It was attempting to industrialize and to deprofessionalize teaching faculty. I was being directed to distribute knowledge in an efficient manner without question or discussion. In the Professor of Teaching stream, exploration, criticality, and creativity were not being promoted. Focus was on the technical, pragmatic aspect of pedagogy.

As I reflected on my situation, I recognized the inequity that reigned in the public educational sphere. In particular, I wondered about the unconscious, invisible cloak of uncontested cultural capital covering the value-laden middle-class European curricula and, in parallel present in scholarly culture. Despite the socioeconomic and cultural diversity in classrooms and the presence of empathetic and caring pedagogy, the primacy of traditional Eurocentric curricula and a transmission-style approach to teaching and learning were being strongly implemented. I pondered the lack of intellectual resources relating to the students' ancestries in the classroom. Was the wealth of aboriginal and/or South East Asian epistemology, traditions, and literature present in the educational environment? For example, students in grade 7 were reading the novel that I learned in my own grade 7 years, set in an urban, monocultural, unilingual North American environment. Within the context of an elementary school with a growing aboriginal population, First Nations pedagogy based on the Medicine Wheel of Learning, describing the four components of a balanced lifestyle: the intellectual, physical, emotional, and spiritual and addressing a person's location in relation to individual, family, community, and nation, could have been situated as an important component of the educational objectives (Preston, 2011). Readings, movies, and songs from South East Asian classical and popular culture could have been incorporated into subject areas. This observation juxtaposed with my self-exploration and self-realization allowed me, once again, to reflect on the power and the privilege of the cultural capital and cultural habitus being reproduced and validated in the context of public schooling and postsecondary education.

As I came back to my academic practice, I understood that by applying critical theory to practice and praxis, I could precipitate disrupt, interrogate the status quo, provide positive role-modeling, choose culturally relevant resources, use culturally responsive pedagogy, and attempt to develop inclusive, democratic habits of mind in my students and in my practice. Reflecting on my career in the Professor of Teaching stream, I also realized the impact my voice, my words, and my experiences had on my students and colleagues.

HABITS OF MIND

Grant and Gibson (2011) recognize the importance of teacher education to go beyond the technocratic-rational knowledge to instill "habits of mind" (p. 31). Accordingly habits of mind allow teachers to learn about the impact of cultural knowledge, socially contextual knowledge, content knowledge, and pedagogical tools to improve practice. This approach promotes a vision of inquiry based on examination and interrogation. This musing focused on my role as an educator in a preservice teacher education program. Acknowledging the socioeconomic–cultural disparity between teacher candidates and their urban students, I reflected on improvements to my practice and professional aspirations: How I can bring future educators to understand the aspirations, life trajectories, and outcomes of students in marginalized contexts? How can the university come to understand the marginalization and deskilling foisted on teaching faculty? Specifically, in what ways can I, as a university educator, interrogate the normalcy of privilege, socioeconomic disparity, and the complex dimensions of scholarly and societal life that are re-created and reproduced? In what ways can I engage senior administration in discussions relating to equity and parity between professors and professors of teaching? These initial questions instigated my desire to unpack the invisible weight of power and privilege (McIntosh, 1989) in my practice and disrupt academia's conceptions of teaching and learning. Through the juxtaposition of self-study and critical pedagogy, change, growth, and development had become integral components of the transformative pedagogy that I was embarking on.

REFLECTIVE COMMUNITIES OF PRACTICE

As the self-study drew to a natural conclusion, I recognized the changes that I had instinctively wanted to bring to my practice and now, based on my career progression, would implement. I contemplated my practice through the lens of Bourdieu's (1977, 1991) assertion that schools legitimize the privileging of dominant discourses to the detriment of the multiplicity of alternative perspectives. How would I, within dominant academic discourse, validate democratic and equitable practice for all professors? Since this type of transformative work cannot occur in isolation, I realized that it would be important to develop a reflective community of practice between interdisciplinary university educators. For example, Sullivan and Rosin (2008) suggest a new agenda for higher education by shaping the mind for practice.

Within the context of the professional practice of teachers, they carefully considered the role of theoretical and professional knowledge in higher education. Recognizing the need for change in teaching and learning in postsecondary, an interdisciplinary four-person study group was formed to discuss how liberal arts disciplines should be oriented toward careers of professional practice. Acknowledging the role of philosophy and its relationship to social understanding, this valuable initiative provided the impetus to change the campus-wide perceptions regarding the professional practice of teachers. Reflecting on how I would shape a mind for practice, I focused on the centrality of the concept of *practical reasoning* in initial training. By doing so, my practice migrated away from the analysis of educational curriculum and policy toward a philosophical, self-reflective narrative emphasizing the social understanding of race, class, and gender and the ensuing disruption of preconceived notions of teaching and learning. Shifting from Eurocentric curricula and traditional scholarly conceptions of scholarship, I was able to embrace multiple perspectives of teaching and learning with a focus on indigenous knowledge and the ever-growing cultural and linguistic diversity of North American society. When supported by critically conscious communities, teacher education can generate rigorous, intellectual praxis favoring the development of situated best practice. By virtue of critical reflection focusing on my marginalized career path, I recognized that university identities are deeply implicated in classical European traditions of teaching and learning, that community-based service learning experiences, cross-cultural field experiences, and collaborative initiatives between practitioners and interdisciplinary university professors are important initiatives to counter the existing status quo about teaching faculty in universities.

CONCLUSION

In keeping with Sleeter and Milner's call for a "solidly situated broader self-study literature" (qtd. in Ball & Tyson, 2011, p. 95), this analysis of teaching, research, and service has allowed me to come full circle by revisiting my former experiences with marginalization and otherness in elementary and middle schools and situating them within my professional and academic context. As Gay (2003) stated previously, "who we are as people determines the personality of our teaching" (p. 5). Like the oft-quoted Palmer (1997) by virtue of this self-study nuanced with critical pedagogy, *I teach, do research, and do service based on who I am.* I am, first and foremost, a teacher educator, and second, a researcher. In Kanpol's (2010) words, I am a transformative scholar practitioner. Spending time in an urban school made me aware of the power and privilege afforded to university educators in schools. Yet as a teacher educator, I recognized the technocratic and dominant-infused elements of my teaching while acknowledging the deskilling process that was taking place in my own career. I decided to actively commit to pursuing and engaging in questions about the reproduction of structure, power, and privilege in educational practice on campus and off campus. I intended to shed the shackles of academic constraints and deskilling of teaching faculty by validating the long-lost *other*, *hidden* voices clamoring in schools and in teacher education. My critical self-reflection clarified my personal and professional career progression as a Professor of Teaching engaged in constructing authentic and critical knowledge bases. Samaras, Hicks, and Garvey Berger (2007) state that formative contextualized lived experiences influence how we think about teaching. However, this power and privilege did not translate back to my university life. On campus, despite my tenured status, I was marginalized and othered into the teaching stream. I was told repeatedly not to think, not to question, and definitely not to do research. Despite my professorial aspirations, I was deskilled of my critical and creative potential. This reflection provided a powerful mechanism to explore the suffocating campus-wide policies that seek to annihilate intellectual autonomy. Self-study within the lens of critical pedagogy provided not only a reflection of issues relating to my work as a public intellectual, and to my professional identity, but also a methodology that promotes reform of normative practices and the emergence of innovative scholarly cultures. By virtue of this validation, professors of teaching, as transformative scholar practitioners, possess the ability to shape and explore the influences of institutional benchmarks in conceptualizing tenure and promotion.

This chapter has offered teacher educators a praxis-oriented, critical approach to conceiving and developing the public intellectual, academic identity, and service in the twenty-first century. As stated by Sullivan and Rosin (2008), critical reflection and engaged action within theoretical and institutionalized contexts can serve as platforms to generate knowledge transformation. At a time when neoliberal market-driven mandates are informing university educational policy, it is important to keep critical visions and practices alive and to evade deskilling attempts brought forth by academic hierarchies.

CHAPTER TWO

Dwelling Artfully in the Academy

Walking on Precarious Ground

PAMELA RICHARDSON

Wherever you stand,
Be the soul of that place.

—Rumi

In this chapter, I engage in a living and poetic inquiry into my experience as an instructor recently and contingently employed in a faculty newly driven to become research intensive. I consider the possibilities and tensions that arise from engaging with poetic awareness in this setting. As we proceed in our academic careers, we desire largely to maintain the liveliness of our creative and intellectual gifts as scholars and educators, and we seek to inspire these in our teacher candidates and graduate students toward deep, engaged, and transformative learning communities. As such, I draw on notions of gift economy as a necessary context for mindful, artful, and living inquiry practices as an alternative to the current knowledge economy that shapes the culture of educational scholarship.

In the latter half of my doctoral work, before I completed my degree and returned to the mainland of British Columbia for work at a university, I lived on Vancouver Island on an acreage replete with towering firs and graceful arbutus. At the back of my property there was a deer path that traced a gentle line through the temperate rainforest. The several adjoining acreages were owned by a Japanese company who had sought to build a retirement village complete with an artificial lake. They were denied permits yet not before they had clear cut half the land. My collie pup and I would follow this faint deer path through the remaining forest on these undeveloped properties. We would scamper over fallen mossy logs, climb through ever-shifting tangles of purple loosestrife, and meander across wildflower meadows before arriving at the next occupied property with a small white stucco house about a kilometer away. Even though this house was on five acres traversed by a ravine with us on the far side, the resident dog always knew we were tromping about her extended backyard and would raise the alarm. It was here we would turn back.

I evoke the rainforest deer path to invite its lushness and unruliness, its end-less organic curves and its many ways of expressing green, into my mind's eye. Walking daily in this place not only nurtured my ability to work in less linear, strictly rational, and ordered ways but it seemed to necessitate this outpouring. My academic path became less linear and ordered during these years of forest walking. Or perhaps, rather, the artifice of external order fell away and I trusted more in the emergent nature of things (Stewart, 2005). Consciousness is shaped by habit and place, and attending to metaphors both obvious and subtle helps us observe and understand how our minds connect and structure our experiences. Speaking from the field of cognitive poetics, Verdonk (2005) writes,

> Metaphor, metonymy and other figures are no longer seen as an embellishment of language to create a particular stylistic effect, resulting from a process of objective thinking of an in-dependent mind; rather they are seen as a reflection of how people *construe* their knowledge and experience of the world around them. (p. 236)

It was through walking daily in this semi-wilderness that I conceived of my aca-demic writing and research less trammeled by conventional forms. I was able to conceptualize my research, which is situated in the conventional fields of Special and Gifted Education, in arts-based and poetic terms (Irwin, 2004; Leggo, 2008; Neilsen, 2008).

I do not wish to idealize this time, though. While there, I taught full-time as a sessional instructor in a faculty of education at a nearby univeristy, worked as a research assistant, and wrote my dissertation. Despite my love for rainforests and tall trees, I felt out of my element in this rural community where I had recently bought a home. While my walks were outwardly idyllic, inside my mind stormed with thoughts and worries about my future, my finances, my marriage difficulties, doubts and insecurities about my research, and ongoing thoughts about my rela-tionships with colleagues and students – the usual. Still, it was a place so different from the stratified and hierarchical context of the university, and from the grids of the cities where I had always lived, that it served undoubtedly as a powerful counterbalance and alternative to its ways.

As a researcher and educator with commitments to living and mindful inquiry (Bentz & Shapiro, 1998; Meyer, 2010) through interpretive, arts-based, and par-ticipatory forms of research, the quality of my lived experiences and perceptions are formative aesthetic conditions inextricable from my writing and scholarship (Hirshfield, 1997; Varela, Thompson, & Rosch, 1991). Bai (2005) cautions that

> [t]he most important element in inquiry is what the inquirer brings to the process of inquiry: alert and expansive consciousness, sensitivity and receptivity to people and situations, the ability to feel authentically and strongly, the capacity for sustained investigations, creative impulses, imaginative capacities for trying out different "realities," and vitality and enthusiasm. It is well to remember that an inquiry is no longer a living inquiry when the inquirer has abstracted his or her subjectivity out of the content and process of the inquiry. (p. 47)

For this reason, through my teaching and research I seek out and seek to nurture contexts that support open, relational, and imaginative living processes.

> Or, at least this is what I wish to do.

It is Sunday morning. I am in line at a coffee shop, my shoulder bag stuffed with my laptop and too many books.

> "Hey, Pamela. Are you having your usual?" Lucy calls over.
> "Yes, please. A decaf americano," I say.

I am spending a lot of time at this coffee shop. I live alone and even though I have been here a year, I know few people in this town where I relocated last summer for work. I do not have much time to nurture a social life and recognize that apart from friendship with colleagues this is a need that is not being fulfilled. As a full-time instructor in an education faculty, my energy is consumed by my teaching and all the work that goes into high-quality course development and facilitating deep learning and supportive community for teacher candidates and teachers. I also work hard to maintain the thread of my research and scholarship so that I remain competitive for tenure-track positions. I have found that writing with my laptop in a coffee shop provides that unique blend of social contact and privacy that I cannot get either at my house or in my office at the university; it is, possibly, a kind of third-space that promises more freedom in my thinking.

I move to a table and plug in, but I do not get to work right away. First, I check my email and then do a quick scan of my Facebook page. Again, this provides a bit of social contact that does not require a lot of time or effort from me. Then there is the fact that it is Sunday morning and I do not *feel* like working. I have been teaching all week in our intensive summer B.Ed. program. To spend a weekend in the middle of July working on a chapter before returning to another full week of teaching does not give me the rest that I need.

Still, I turn the Wi-Fi signal off on my laptop so that I am not tempted by those email alerts flashing at the bottom of my screen. I open a blank document. What am I going to say? What is my intent with this chapter? I stare at the screen entirely unsure. The intensity of my schedule in the past year has not allowed for much time to pause and reflect. When I try to identify a moment that deserves more reflection – a "stop moment" (Appelbaum, 1995; Fels & Belliveau, 2008) in my experience of working "artfully or poetically" in the academy – I draw a blank. Possibly this is the white-out of an avalanche; there has been too much that has happened at too quick of a pace. Mixed with my feelings of uncertainty is an omnipresent feeling of pressure so familiar that I barely recognize it as a being distinct from my sense of self, as being "not me." It is an inner hum that is sometimes low and slow, and other times higher and faster. This is most likely the reason my mind is blank. I have a lot of other work to do today to get ready for my upcoming teaching week, and I cannot spend too much time working on this promised chapter.

> I must come to
> a sudden stop
> to quickly
> produce a piece
> aboout slowing down.
>
> I feel
> I must
> and so,
> I do.
>
> Stillpoint.
> Here I am.

Sadness wells up in my throat. I feel like crying. This is an impossible place and it is where I find myself most often. It has been a while since I have stopped. How do I maintain a poetic and artful orientation to research when I am too busy to pause? I depend on mindful attention and heartful attunement to capture the underlying poetry of teaching, learning, and living situations. My work is predicated on attending to language and articulating deeper connections and relationships that underlie being and knowing. How do I find stillpoints in the flow of activity to let experience percolate up into my consciousness? Hirshfield (1997) says,

> Every good poem begins in language awake to its own connections – language that hears itself and what is around it.… It begins, that is, in the body and mind of concentration. By concentration, I mean a particular state of awareness: penetrating, unified, and focused, yet also permeable and open. (p. 3)

I have not been, in the words of one of my dear mentors, "living poetically" (Leggo, 2005) and fear losing touch with this quality of mind. Leggo (2008) says that

> Poetry is a way of knowing, being and becoming.… The poet-researcher seeks to live attentively in the moment, to know the momentousness of each moment, to seek to enter lived experiences with a creative openness to people and experiences and understandings. (p. 168)

This tension between the academic autobahn and the deer path that sustains my poetic awareness compels an inauthentic move to disembodied abstraction (Bai, 2005) where I risk *mimicking* a living and poetic inquiry so that I can merge successfully into an academic career. I am beginning to fear that this may be the real risk.

The academy needs poets but do poets need the academy?

Hyde (1979/2007) explores how art and creativity thrive under conditions made scarce by market-driven capitalism. He delves into the disconnect that exists between public service, pure science, and artistic practices on the one hand, and common forms of earning a living in a neoliberal economy on the other. He says,

> there are categories of human enterprise that are not well organized or supported by market forces. Family life, religious life, public service, pure science, and of course much artistic practice.... Any community that values these things will find nonmarket ways to organize them. It will develop gift-exchange institutions dedicated to their support. (p. 370)

What Hyde means by gift-exchange institutions are spaces wherein work can be freely envisioned, created, and shared without the kinds of accounting measures, analytics, and quid pro quo arrangements that define academic culture. I am sometimes in awe at how academic structures and systems have bent and reformed themselves in a supplicating kowtow to accountability measures, which sharply dictate and delimit what counts as valuable research, productivity, and knowledge based on narrow epistemological claims. In their exploration of the various economic ghosts or presences that haunt the knowledge economy, and those forms of exchange, such as gift economies and libidinal economies, that support poetic and artful endeavors, Kenway, Bullen, Fahey, and Robb (2006) ask,

> What role is there for knowledge which is incommensurate with the knowledge economy's economic logic and its handmaidens science and technology?... [W]ill the knowledge economy seek to extinguish the illumination [art] provides, just as Scrooge did the ghost's light? (p. 77)

The function of gifts – both material gifts as well as inner gifts of inspiration and talent – are that through being shared and circulated they create social cohension and strengthen relationships within a community. "It is the cardinal difference between gift and commodity exchange that a gift establishes a feeling-bond between two-people, while the sale of commodity leaves no necessary connection" (Hyde, 1979/2007, p. 72). As a teacher educator and educational researcher my work is steeped in relationship building and requires mindful attention to the complexities of learning in community. This work withers under the exchange values and analytics of the marketplace, which seeks to quantify productivity and effectiveness in narrow terms through course evaluations and generalizable research findings. So, when gifts are evaluated with the wrong metrics they lose their vitality and their connective function. The power of gifts to connect individuals is destroyed when they are appraised with an accountant's eye:

> The hegemony of the market can undermine the possibility of gift exchange, the esemplas-
> tic powers can be destroyed by an overvaluation of analytic cognition, song can be silenced
> by self-consciousness, and the plenitude of the imagination can be lost to the scarcity of
> logic. (Hyde, 1979/2007, p. 201)

Often the work of constructing and justifying one's worth within academic terms is an exercise in technical and myopic autobiography via CVs and reports. This kind of analytic self-scrutiny is anathema to the flourishing of authentic gifts and talents, and it is kryptonite to their "esemplastic powers." It is a context of freedom that enables a gift's liveliness, and we need ways of valuing and relating to our work that enable our gifts to authentically emerge and thrive.

The foundation that supports a poetic and art-based inquiry is thus similar to an iceberg. The poetic or artful extrusion in the form of the poem is just the tip. Most of the work is below the surface. Somedays this vital process within me is quite silent and submerged. Drawing on the work of Lyotard, who used psychoan-nalytic theory to explore the unconcious desires of economic disccourses, Kenway, Bullen, Fahey, and Robb (2006) explain how capitalist systems seek to channel, use, and regulate libidinal, unconscious energies and emotional intensities. They say: "Lyotard describes capital as a 'disposition' or social structure that shares sim-ilarities with the Ego or consciousness insofar as its function is to modulate and moderate, repress and exploit libidinal energies" (p. 77). In this view, poetry sur-faces as a disruptive force powered by emotional intensity incommensurate with a capitalist knowledege economy, which, not finding the exchange value of poetic knowledge, discards it.

In this context might my sense of a submerged poetic pulse – or the anxious drawing of a blank that I spoke of earlier – be a defensive mechanism that protects my emotional and poetic knowing from exploitation, rejections, or co-optation in a capitalist system? "Intensities are free-flowing impulses characterized by their displaceability and resistance to closure, which return from the repressed and rup-ture the stability of conscious organizations" (Lyotard, 1993, p. xiii, as cited in Kenway, Bullen, Fahey, & Robb, p. 77). And, "the unconsious is what is there and yet hidden... a blank space in a visible text" (Foucault, 1973, p. 374, as cited in Kenway, Bullen, Fahey, & Robb, p. 77).

Sometimes I cry or laugh or get excited or dejected when I write as I surface emotions that are formative to my understanding and need to be processed and released. Like an iceberg, if I flip the process and proportions over to empha-size output and performance over authentic depth of awareness regarding my embodied reality, I am baseless and essentially sunk – as a human, as an edu-cator, and as an inquirer. To produce sufficient work that emerges authentically from awareness cultivated through mindful living and artful practices is the goal. Hirshfield (1997) reminds us that it is the tension and friction with life itself that draws and focuses the poet's attention. She says: "Art… is thought that has been concentrated in just this way: honed and shaped by a silky attention brought to bear on the recalcitrant matter of earth and life. We seek in art the elusive intensity by which it knows" (p. 5).

To escape my precarious and marginal academic position I must secure a foothold and begin to scale a university hierarchy rife with economic exchanges. A common discourse maintains that it is only through scaling this wall that one locates on the other side a space of affordance and freedom that enables more creative work. Artistic engagement is not a viable pathway through the academy but potentially a reward for time served. We make our path by walking through (Varela, 1987), and indeed our wall by climbing, and this making is fundamentally collective and mutually constitutive – a co-poeisis. I seek, thus, in the words of Hyde (1979/2007), "nonmarket ways to organize" my relationship to my scholarship, students, and colleagues as the fundament for my academic life.

My wish is for a living and mindful scholarship of artful relations that comprise an alternative to those forces that would break down imaginative action and thought in the name of pseudo-educational discourses based in marketplace rationales. I seek here to understand what it means to dwell artfully and poetically as a researcher and practitioner – or attempt to do so – in a twenty-first-century Canadian Faculty of Education.

Arts-based educational research, or the use of artistic practices, including the literary arts, to inquire into, represent, and transform lived experiences of teaching and learning broadly conceived, emerged in the 1980s and 1990s through the work of Eliot Eisner (e.g., Eisner, 1981, 1991, 1993, 1995, 1997) and Thomas Barone (e.g. Barone, 2008; Barone & Eisner, 1997). Arts-based inquiry methodologies have since then developed through the efforts of a diverse community of scholar-practitioners across disciplinary (education, nursing, sociology, anthropology, business, psychology, sport, women's studies), artistic (visual arts, music, dance, literary arts, theater), and national boundaries (for examples, see Knowles & Cole, 2008). Through the use of arts-based inquiry practices I give rise to nontechnical conceptions of knowledge that are intrinsically relational, situated, and emotional. Further, this artistic process and practice surfaces my situation as a researcher as I make sense of my ongoing experiences of learning and knowing within my field. "A/r/tography is steeped in the practices of artist-educators committed to ongoing living inquiry and it is this inquiry that draws forth the identity of a researcher" (Irwin & Springgay, 2008, p. xxv).

An arts-based inquiry forms a different relationship to research questions and method than a traditional research process. Traditionally, research begins with a question or questions and then determines an appropriate method for answering the questions within a relative degree of certainty. While more questions may emerge along the way, a researcher inquires to argue or prove a central hypothesis, conjecture, or proposition, while acknowledging gaps in their certainty and further work that needs to be done. Within an arts-based conception of research, the practice of art making itself shapes the nature and direction of the inquiry. Through engaging in an artistic or poetic process, the inquirer-poet unearths questions and surfaces connections, which make visible aspects of their experiences of meaning-making. In these terms, research is perceived, say Irwin and Springgay (2008), "as a disposition for knowledge creation" (p. xxiii). And, there is "an evolution of questions within the living inquiry processes of the practitioner" (p. xxiii). As an arts-based inquirer, I am not separate from the subject, the questions, or the inquiry process. I am immersed within the inquiry and my gestures or practices (writing, thinking, conversing, teaching) shape my path. This path in turn shapes my practices, and this reflexive interplay or dance creates a complex of meaning. My form or expression creates and expresses my shifting relationships and position in the world. My work as an arts-based inquirer is to artfully represent aspects or moments of this ongoing process. Irwin and Springgay (2008) say,

> A/r/tography is a living practice, a life creating experience examining our personal, political and/or professional living. Is uses a fluid orientation within… contiguous relationships…. Its rigour comes from its continuous reflective and reflexive stance to engagement, analysis and learning. (p. xxix)

Interpretive, poetic, and artful forms of inquiry that invite emobdied ways of knowing and make visible the self as central to sense-making are still denigrated and devalued in today's knowledge economy in relation to research that claims to offer objective, rational, and transcendent truths. Beneath this denigration lies fear of its power to shift one's relation to accepted reality and structures as organized through status-quo social arrangements of gender, class, ethnicity, and ability (Dinnerstein, 1976); fear of the emotions that surface when one's body is attended to; fear of too closely examining the quality of one's self, life, and one's mortal condition. Boler (1999) says, "What we are faced with in the course of the most ordinary lifetime is terrifying. The desire to order chaos through simplified schemas, to ward off the felt dangers of ambiguity, seems perhaps more 'human' a characteristic than any other" (p. 175). We seek to define, tame, and discipline emotions in education, not invite them into the driver's seat. To do so is dangerous driving on the autobahn indeed. Do I really want to sit in the middle of my experience and know what occupies my mind and heart as I careen along in my academic career? Do I want to engage in "writing that pays attention to the body, always full of energy and determination to get at the heart of the matter, with matters of the heart, often filled with pain"? (Chambers, Hasebe-Ludt, & Leggo, 2012, p. xxiii). For me, there is no better and more important way to live, learn, and teach. Yet "the educator who endeavors to rattle complacent cages, who attempts to 'wrest us anew' from the threat of conformism, undoubtedly faces the treacherous ghosts of the others fears and terrors, which in turn evoke one's own demons" (Boler, 1999, p. 175).

One needs an alert and sensitive awareness to feel into one's own and others' situations beneath the layers of our particular embeddness within cultural and social phenomena. This is an awareness that is cultivated through practice. Aoki (2005) says we need to find ways to "set aside these layers that press upon us and move to indwell in the earthy place where we experience daily life with our colleagues and teacher candidates, and begin our search for the 'isness' of teaching, for the being of teaching" (p. 190). Poetry at its best provides us with a mainline to this kind of awareness. That is one of the functions of poetic attention and expression. The implications of educational inquiry that progresses without this fundamental poetic awareness frightens me, as I believe like Audre Lorde (1985) that "poetry is not a luxury" if we want ethical and just educational scholarship.

Poetry is *not* a luxury. It is the antidote to the disconnection between action and belief. This famous phrase from Lorde has been abstracted for me now, though. It has been too long since I have read even a bit of *Sister Outsider* (Lorde, 1985) from which it comes. Poetry increasingly does feel like a luxury in my academic life even though I do not believe it is. If it seems this way it is due to its scarcity, not because it is inessential.

Still, here is what really happens: Back in the coffeeshop where I am sitting – an ache in my sacroiliac joint from the hard chair – I click on my Wi-Fi connection. I do not have time to go find the book with the Lorde quote. If I still even own it is in a storage locker with most of my possessions. I complete a Web search for "poetry is not a luxury Lorde," and I find on the blog "On Being with Krista Tippett" an excerpted page, which includes the famous line. Lorde (1985) says:

> poetry is not a luxury. It is a vital necessity of our existence.... Poetry is the way we help give name to the nameless so it can be thought... carved from the rock experiences of our daily lives. As they become known to and accepted by us, our feelings and the honest exploration of them become sanctuaries and spawning grounds for the most radical and daring of ideas. They become a safe-house for that difference so necessary to change and the conceptualization of any meaningful action. (p. 36)

I have abstracted even the quote above; the original quote as written by Lorde (1985) actually begins with: "For women poetry is not a luxury." It is a call for women to use the power of poetic engagement to imagine a new world from their lived locations – to use the knowledge of their emotional bodies as the fuel for revolution. "The innovation that the avant-garde supposes is qualitatively different from innovation in the knowledge economy, above all because it is political in the sense of responsibility, justice and resistance" (Kenway, Bullen, Fahey, & Robb,

2006, p. 77). I have begun to feel keenly that the fight for the right to be human and humane within systems and to imagine and make real new possibilities is one that women, men, and those who feel comfortable in neither gender category must engage in together.

I check my word count on my paper and feel better. My anxious inner hum has gone quiet while I am caught in the flow of writing and composing my thoughts. I am being productive. Writing poetry and writing about poetry are two different states but at least they share a long and permeable border. I have been dwelling with my experiences and my felt-sense of the tension between poetic awareness and expected academic production. I am reminded of that religious maxim that encourages one to be *in* the world but not *of* the world (I resist the temptation to do a Web search): Is this the original tension? Is poetic consciousness a way to be *in* the academy without being *of* the academy? What is this work of traveling between these two states? Who am I if I do this?

I do feel *in* and somewhat *of* the academy lately as I race from one thing to the next and seek to build a career from my contingent, nontenure location. Willinsky (1989) says that those who study teaching and learning need to better "describe the history of the script and set within which the teacher is busily improvising and performing" (p. 252) to better represent the systems and factors at play. I seek to do this through more textured and nuanced representations, and more awareness of my situation in relation to others. Based on Boler's (1999) notion of a pedagogy of discomfort, Wolgemuth and Donohue (2006) suggest an inquiry of discomfort. They say that "the aim of an inquiry of discomfort is to identify and promote an intentional and conscious shift from dualistic, categorical, and entrenched positionality to a more ambiguous engagement with social reality" (p. 1024). These practices helps us to work in that in-between space that rejects dualities and disconnections between self, other, feelings, and experiences toward a more complex engagement with our social reality. Boler (1999) cautions that

> the path of understanding, if it is not to "simplify," must be tread gently. Yet if one believes in alternatives to the reductive binaries of good and evil, "purity and corruption," one is challenged to invite the other, with compassion and fortitude, to learn to see things differently, no matter how perilous the course for all involved. (p. 176)

Appelbaum (1995) refers to this space as "the stop." It is "the element... that... breaks an on rushing momentum and opens experience to another point of view... [S]uch moments illuminate and nurture shifts in perspective and provide the impetus or sparks for reflexive consciousness to emerge" (p. ix). I seek thus to "stop" in this tension that has split my awareness so that I may re-infuse my living inquiry with my subjective and embodied presence in such a way that I better illuminate my context. Poetic awareness and arts-based approaches to knowing open portals into what Marcuse (1964) terms a "rebellious subjectivity," or, a dimension of experience particular to individuals positioned on the fringes of a system, which facilitates critical stances. My perspective on academic culture is from the margins and I also engage in marginalized forms of inquiry. This "marginal" position is an essential and powerful position from which to understand collective experiences and situations, and from which to take action. It is an essential perspective toward a more critical reflexivity and engaged pedagogy.

I am conscious as I write this chapter that my dean will be reading and responding to it. I have been wondering how to write about my perspective on what it means to be a scholar and practitioner without making this about me and about her. Again, I am seeing this need to abstract myself and another, to distance from my subjectivity out of fear – not fear of my dean but fear of what I might reveal about myself that would make me incommensurable with the expected role the academy desires of me. So, instead, I seek to stand in the center of my experience and find refuge in this stance. I seek a stillpoint where I can be not like a tree rooted but like a deer poised, attuned and ready to leap into action.

Doe a deer almost grown
still on the shoulder, eyes fixed.
What do you do when you see a dead doe on the road?
While piano pulses from the radio,
Partita in B minor by Bach, and
clouds rest in the arms of evergreens
with ghost-like lingering, and even
oily exhaust from the old Tempo
in front rises into oblivion.

Race up concrete hills in the rain
two stairs for daily exercise,
press down tangled hair with quick palms
to meet teacher candidates,
arrive breathless but say:
slow down on the road,
watch the edge of the forest,
pay attention to the doe emerging,
the live one.

CHAPTER THREE

Ideology, Performativity, and the University

CATHERINE BROOM

Within contemporary discourses, the concept of neoliberalism is an ideology that influences working conditions in a number of institutions like Faculties of Education through policy, budgets, employment terms, and institutional aims. Emerging from business, neoliberalism is grounded in economic rationalism. It aims to maximize business profits through control of employee and industrial productivity using performance, sales, or production targets. This neoliberal rhetoric values market-driven actions, consumer satisfaction and choice, and economic profit, and it applies business practices to the regulation of other social institutions. In schools, its techniques include accountability, choice, standardized testing, and public rankings.

A number of writers including Ball (1999, 2003, 2006) and Apple (2006) describe these as having negative results on teachers and students in both the UK and the United States. Apple states, for example, that rather than focusing on student learning, schools aim to improve their school's ranking by attempting to attract "good" students and directing resources away from special-needs students. Teachers teach to standardized, fact-based tests and do not focus on developing important abilities such as critical thinking, which are not considered in their performative assessment criteria. Creative and innovative teaching practice decline as these are also not assessed. Further, as students have varying amounts of capital with which to negotiate the system and parents with more social, economic, and cultural capital can move their children at will within the system, inequalities in schools rise. Accordingly, control through performative means are a function of "a concern for external supervision, regulation, and external judgement of performance" (Apple, 2006, p. 478) that often accompany a devalued belief in the professional ability and judgment of educators.

In keeping with the concept of contested sites in education, this chapter discusses the impact that neoliberalism has had and is having on Faculty of Education professors through Ball's theory of performativity. After describing this theory and introducing a short review of the history of tenure and promotion, the findings of a research study based on performativity in Canadian universities are presented. The ensuing discussion focuses on the impact of performativity on professors' identities and thus their conceptions and actions toward what it means to be a public intellectual and to engage in service. The chapter concludes with recommendations that consider alternative possibilities to that of performativity that provide spaces for authenticity, mentoring and nurturing communities, and individual and social flourishing (Broom, 2010).

THEORY OF PERFORMATIVITY

Recognizing that critiques of the impact of neoliberalism on university professors draw on the conceptual work of theorists such as Lyotard, Foucault, and Ball, the following offers a brief summary of each of these authors' works.

Lyotard

Lyotard argued that education today no longer aims for goals such as individual freedom but rather has been co-opted to serve the goals of the state and the global marketplace. In the postmodern "knowledge economy," knowledge is conceptualized as a commodity: It is legitimized by its utility, by being of use in society. This knowledge is sought by those with power to increase their power. University performance managers thus advocate for the economic value of the knowledge universities create to the knowledge economy – they argue that universities add "economic value" to society (Duncan, n.d.). As a result, universities no longer fulfill their purpose of knowledge creation for its intrinsic value but, rather, have been re-conceptualized within neoliberal discourse. University managers regulate knowledge- and human capital producing university professors through economic incentives and performance targets (Duncan, n.d.). This system requires particular types of people, those constituted through discourse and modern education, as discussed by Foucault (Marshall, 1999).

Foucault

Foucault's work explored the connections between power and knowledge (Bai, Bartley, & Broom, 2007). He argued that varying times and places have had different discourses, that is, distinct ways of understanding the world, which were connected to knowledge formation and power. Power, for Foucault, is a complex framework of interrelations between concepts and legitimate authority. Knowledge is power, forming people's lived reality. For example, the rise of the modern state changed the manner in which control was exercised over people. In a Monarchical state, power was made visible through the grandeur of the monarch and dramatic public spectacles, such as executions. This form of control allowed for pockets of resistance, when one was away from the eyes of the monarch and his aides. With the collapse of monarchies and the rise of the modern state, control and power shifted to more subtle means: "hierarchical observation, normalizing judgement, and their combination in a procedure that is specific to it, the examination" (Foucault, 2006, p. 124).

Control Through Observation, Examination, and Comparison

Since knowledge is conceived as a powerful commodity, observation becomes a type of control through visibility, the ability to see what others are doing. The panopticon is the most well-known example: By removing "blind" spots – by making all visible – individuals could be effectively controlled (and become self-regulating), with little need for violent public displays. Normalizing judgment is the setting up of a standard of behavior or achievement to which all individuals are compared, "so that they might all be like one another" (Foucault, 2006, p. 120). They are classified as "satisfactory" if they meet the standard, and "unsatisfactory" if not. Standardized marking criteria are an example. Schools use all three forms of control: teachers observe and evaluate students and compare them to standards, or what we might call grade expectations. The exam is one of the main methods used to classify the perceived quality of students, assessing some students as successful and others as failures, with real consequences for these students. These marks "constitute" or shape the individual's identity by assigning him or her a certain value based on external criteria. Similar means are also used to control and evaluate university professors' work.

Lyotard's conception of knowledge as validated through performativity, or its usefulness in postmodern, neoliberal societies, forms one conceptual basis for Ball's work. Foucault's discussion of the discourse of modern states in which control occurs through observation, examination, and comparison forms the second conceptual basis of Ball's theory of performativity.

Ball and Performativity

In Ball's theory of performativity, mechanisms of control, such as visibility and standards, are used to control behaviors with the aim of increasing efficiency. The aim is to compete successfully in the global marketplace. Ball (2006) describes performativity as

> a technology, a culture and mode of regulation, or even a system of "terror" in Lyotard's words, that employs judgements, comparisons, and displays as means of control, attrition and change. The performances, of individual subjects of organizations, serve as measure of productivity or output. They stand for, encapsulate or represent the worth, quality, or value or an individual or organization. (p. 693)

Performativity is manifested in several ways including through language and commercialization. Language is illustrated in educational policy in documents such as Standards of Practice and in Lyotard's conception of words that structure meaning (Ball, 2002). Commercialization of education occurs through the development of materials that consider students and their parents to be "customers" and aim to attract them to particular schools. These mechanisms cause fear and fragmentation as people are forced to demonstrate that they meet government-set standards through the production of particular documents, such as reports (Ball, 2002).

Performativity establishes a culture of control in a manner similar to Foucault's concept of visibility. Fear of public humiliation is its effective driver. It influences both individuals and institutions. Ball provides examples: The ranking of schools and universities according to standardized tests scores is changing their practices as schools and universities feel pressure to "compete successfully" for students, and the evaluation of professors for tenure is affecting their behaviors. For professors, the aim is to appear successful through strategically developed "promotion texts" (Ball, 2006, p. 699). For universities, the aim is to fabricate the appearance of meeting their clients' demands, for example, by using teaching evaluations to rate the perceived "quality" of the instructor and to engage in behaviors that will increase the public ranking of the university.

Assessments and reviews can cause fear and uncertainty and thus result in particular behaviors – performances – from the individual and the institution. These fabricated behaviors, aiming for security, can affect individuals' identities and lead to the "possibility that commitment, judgement, and authenticity within practice are sacrificed for impression" (Ball, 2006, p. 695). While some individuals manage to maintain authenticity by staying true to their own beliefs and practices within the system (Ball, 2003), others do not. By acting in particular performative ways, some individuals lose connection with themselves and, thus, can come to feel emptiness inside. Performances, in other words, can cause inauthenticity and thus negatively affect professional and personal identities.

Non-conformance, as Westheimer (2003) writes, can have serious consequences for job security. This loss of authentic identity may affect professors' conceptions of both the public intellectual and service, for these may only be engaged with by many professors to the extent that they are recognized within performance criteria.

Performativity, to sum up, is the actions that result from the discourse of neoliberalism, which is present in a number of varied nations around the world (Ball, 1999), including the United States, the UK, and Canada.

Performativity in Canadian Universities

Based on the above discussion, neoliberal ideology is influencing professors' behaviors as they progress through the ranks of tenure and promotion. According to Polster (2009), professors are becoming more individualized (i.e., more self-serving and less community-focused). They are increasingly collaborating with business for grants, which universities value due to their focus on budgets. These grants fund research that often increases business profits (the "usefulness" criteria of performativity according to Lyotard). Further, professors are changing their teaching practice by assigning higher grades to all students (Churchill, 2006), termed "grade inflation," as they don't want their students to give them bad teaching evaluations. These changes are due to performance expectations set by university administrators, whose managerial style mirrors that of business managers. These managers focus on financial profitability, budgets, and quantitative data analysis. Performance evaluations, merit pay, university ranking tables (taken seriously by administration), the tenure and promotion process and criteria, benchmarking, awards, and making comparisons using statistics and ratios are all examples of performativity present in Canadian higher education institutions. These managers also attempt to increase profits through the implementation of lucrative programs, such as international students. Students are seen as "clients," whose customer satisfaction is measured through teaching evaluations.

Despite this theoretical work, little concrete research evidence exists exploring what university professors in Canada think: To what degree do they think performativity exists in Canadian universities? Is it causing a culture of fear that is leading professors to engage in performances and fabrications, and thus to lose authenticity? The next section addresses this dearth in knowledge by exploring to what degree performativity is found in Canadian universities from the perceptions of new, untenured faculty, and comparing these views with those of tenured faculty. As the tenure and promotion process is a central driver of performativity, the next section begins with a brief historical review of the tenure and promotion process to see how it has changed over the last century.

HISTORICAL REVIEW OF TENURE AND PROMOTION

History of Tenure and Promotion in the United States (Youn & Price, 2009)

A period of rapid growth post–World War II led to increasingly complex organizational structures, policies, and procedures in American universities. Tenure and promotion rules and procedures expanded significantly in the 1970s. Tenure and promotion moved from the general university administration/president to faculties and became increasingly more complex. For example, external reviews became a requirement. Policies were copied from other institutions, partly through the move of administrators across universities. Stagnation in population growth rates (and thus student numbers), plus economic downturn, led to stringent competition between higher education schools in the 1980s, and this resulted in changes to faculty working conditions. Professors faced increased pressure to be seen as successful scholars through the production of a strong scholarly output, which aimed to boost the university's status generally. In the 1980s and especially 1990s, pressure for publications rose greatly and institutions increasingly attempted to specialize to differentiate themselves from competitors.

Further, race, gender, and class play a role in influencing the rates of tenure and promotion. Wolfinger, Mason, and Goulden (2008), for example, found that women achieve tenure less than men due to the influence of outside factors such as families. Jayakumar, Howard, Allen, and Han (2009) found similar findings for racial minorities due to barriers associated with racism. Similar historical trends to those that occurred in the United States are apparent at one Canadian university, the University of British Columbia.

History of Tenure and Promotion at One Canadian Institution

The University of British Columbia (UBC) in British Columbia, Canada, was founded in 1915 (Whittaker & Ames, 2006). At first, this emergent postsecondary institution had small departments and limited course options. It focused on expanding by recruiting people with the required qualifications. As there was demand for professors, individuals were hired with their PhDs still in progress. According to a history of the anthropology department, which included personal communications with professors who were there in those early years up until the mid-1960s, the university's administration style was informal, benevolent, run by white males, and paternalistic. Tenure and promotion decisions were made by the department head and the university president, and appointment, tenure, and promotion committees did not exist. As the university grew in size and student numbers, and its departments expanded, it increasingly rationalized its processes and procedures for tenure and promotion in a similar manner to that which occurred in other institutions across North America, borrowing policies and procedures from other universities. The 1962 UBC Faculty Handbook mentioned that the Canadian Association of University Teachers had been formed to deal with tenure and promotion at the national level. It was clearly involved at this particular institution as it included a faculty association booklet on tenure and promotion.

Changes are illustrated in the UBC Faculty Handbooks of the 1960s, which are described next. These guides for university professors at UBC began to include tenure and promotion policies. These policies continued to be refined over the century.

UBC Faculty Handbooks

Faculty Handbooks, Tenure and Promotion, 1960 and 1962

Archival research revealed that the 1962 Faculty Handbook was much larger than the 1960 handbook (UBC, 1960). The 1960 Faculty Handbook did not mention tenure and promotion specifically. It focused, mostly, on describing the benefits that faculty received, such as the faculty club and library – perhaps this aimed to attract and retain faculty at the growing university. The 1962 handbook included a new, full section on tenure and promotion (UBC, 1962). It described the three levels of the professoriate and explained that individuals could be hired with or without term. Qualifications were to be measured by "teaching effectiveness" and "scholarly attainments" (UBC, 1962, p. 15). The first could be assessed by colleagues, student interest levels, and reputation, the second by the quality of the candidate's (1) degrees; (2) research, which was demonstrated in publications and awards; and (3) service, which was demonstrated by membership on boards and recognition by professional societies. Mention was made that these criteria could be demonstrated in different ways.

Instructors were assessed on their teaching ability. Assistant professors should demonstrate "successful teaching ability and/or professional experience, together with evidence of scholarly or appropriate professional ability beyond that involved in the completion of academic or professional training" (UBC, 1962, p. 16). In other words, they were to demonstrate potential in their field. The requirements for promotion to associate professor were "not automatic, nor based on years of service alone. It is expected that some assistant professors may not attain this rank" (p. 16). Criteria again focus on teaching, scholarship, and service. The handbook mentioned that promotion to professor was not automatic and depended on being ranked "outstanding."

According to UBC policy, promotion was separated from tenure. Promotion was not given to all faculty and was related to how faculty contributions were assessed. Tenure was given to those who had served for seven years, with five of those years being at the university. Tenure was defined as having one's position "without term" and only being dismissible for "adequate cause," which included financial challenges. The handbook mentioned that, if a person did not receive tenure, he or she was to be given a one-year, final contract. Assessment criteria were not further described or elaborated, except to state that tenure was not necessarily granted if a person's contract went over seven years, and that it could be granted in a shorter time period as well. The person had to be rehired a few times first: Initial appointment and subsequent reappointments were for two years. An associate professor was hired for three years and was given tenure, if rehired, as long as there were no "unusual circumstances" (UBC, 1962, p. 17). Professors were hired with tenure.

The individual was reappointed by the board on the recommendation of the president, who acted on the dean's recommendation. While colleagues were described as playing a role in recommendations, the final authority was given to the dean. It appears that administrators were the main decision makers regarding tenure. This was to be increasingly monitored by the Faculty Association, which issued a handbook supplement in 1963. This supplement stated that contributions could vary and explained that "excellence" was assessed by considering teaching reputation, the quality of research conducted, which should contribute to the "advancement of knowledge," and professional competence. The last was assessed by how well professors advanced knowledge in their fields and how they contributed to their university, community, and nation. Instructors, assistant professors, and associate professors were reviewed yearly.

Faculty Handbook, Tenure and Promotion, 2010

The 2010 handbook is similar to the 1962 handbook, illustrating that performative practices were already in place during the 1960s. Professors are required to demonstrate excellence in teaching, research, and service and are recommended for tenure and/or promotion by the dean with advice from a committee of peers. However, the initial and subsequent reappointments are for three years. Tenure and promotion are applied for prior to the seventh year. One may be granted without the other. Changes include the following: the candidates are asked to provide external references, two of which are used by the dean to inquire into the work of the candidate, along with two additional references chosen by the dean. The handbook also includes more details on the procedures for carrying out the review, and opportunities for the individual to respond to negative recommendations are explained.

General Discussion of Tenure and Promotion Policies

The handbooks demonstrate much similarity in their tenure and promotion criteria. In both cases, the criteria are vague in the extreme and are thus open to interpretation. Consequently, administrators and committee members have much decision-making power. The two handbooks do differ in that the newer handbook has more emphasis on faculty peer review and faculty association input, which aim to ensure a fairer review process, perhaps illustrating that administrators were seen to hold too much power. This would follow a similar historical pattern to that of the United States, described above, where changes related to advocacy on the part of faculty and faculty associations occurred. However, as few specific details are included in the handbooks (such as number of publications), it is difficult to estimate the degree of changes to these criteria. American work states that the criteria became more challenging in the 1970s due to institutional competition and a desire to do well to rank well in the marketplace (a performativity factor). Thus, the requirements for success in publishing and grants increased. This is most likely the case in Canada as well, for Canadian universities have followed a number of general world trends related to universities including (1) competition for students; (2) decreased governmental budgets; (3) pressures to follow neoliberal procedures including accountability; and (4) a belief that efficiency requires quantification and oversight for control of costs and profit maximization (Polster, 2009).

While evidence of more stringent criteria may not be apparent in the faculty handbooks, the research study findings with Faculty of Education professors below help to shed light on this, and on whether this is creating more stress on faculty and, thus, potentially fostering performativity practices by them. As indicated previously, these can affect professors' identities and service work.

RESEARCH STUDY DESCRIPTION

Methodology

Tenured and untenured university professors were invited to participate in the study by email using the Canadian Society for the Study of Education (CSSE) distribution list. The research tool was an anonymous questionnaire filled out online using fluid surveys (www.fluidsurveys.com). Potential participants were informed of the purpose of the study (to explore the extent to which performativity exists in Canadian universities and its effects), the length of time to fill in the survey (10 minutes), and the anonymity of the study. They were then emailed the survey as a link. They demonstrated their consent for the study by filling out the survey form. On the survey, participants were asked questions that aimed to identify if they engaged in performativity-based actions, whether they felt performativity and fear were present at their institution, and whether they felt their institution attempted to mentor its faculty. Space was available to add comments.

The findings were analyzed for themes using a grounded theory approach (Glaser, 1992; Strauss, 1987). The researcher explored the relations between fear (e.g., job insecurity) and the use of performative methods and analyzed the connections between professors' identification of performativity and their beliefs in the amount of mentorship that occurs at their universities.

Limitations of the Research

Findings were collected only from professors who agreed to participate in the study. It is thus possible that they are not representative of faculty's thoughts toward the subject in general in Canada. Often individuals who agree to take part in studies feel strongly for or against the subject, which might mean that the findings are biased toward the margins of professors' views, minimizing the moderate position. The findings, as well, do not consider specific contexts or institutional histories. Further, unfortunately, despite listing the research call in a major national conference distribution list, only 16 people agreed to and participated in the study. This is a small sample size and can't be considered to be representative of the majority viewpoint in Canadian Faculties of Education today. At best, the findings offer a small glimmer of Canadian university professors' views and actions in relation to performativity.

DISCUSSION OF THE RESEARCH FINDINGS

This section begins by discussing the findings for tenure-track professors and then those of tenured professors. Eleven responses were received for tenure-track professors.

Findings for Tenure-Track Professors

All 11 respondents replied that performativity was present at their institutions. They also all agreed that their jobs depended on publishing, grants, and teaching. All but one individual were strategically focusing on getting rehired through actions that illustrate performativity, such as reworking papers or attempting to get grants. The one who answered no was at a research-intensive university. He or she commented that he or she recognizes that the pressure is there, but he or she was not going to let that pressure affect him or her: "I entered academe late in my working life, and have decided that I won't let institutional priorities consume me. I've accepted the possibility that I might have a very short academic career. But I'm going to get pleasure and satisfaction from the work that I am able to do as long as I'm in the academy" (survey respondent, 2013).

Interestingly, and somewhat counter to Ball's work, while respondents agreed that performativity exists and affects their behaviors, only a slight majority (6 out of 11) were fearful about their jobs. Perhaps this is because university professors accept performativity as an aspect of their jobs or because they are being strategic in their actions. Alternatively, perhaps they accept a "what will be, will be" approach, as the one professor commented above. Furthermore, 8 of the 11 respondents didn't feel supported by their faculty. It seems that tenure-track faculty feel that mentorship is missing.

The optional comments are insightful. One person implied that the faculty can be deceptive or unwelcoming: "Nothing is said about having to watch the alliances and to have to keep your epistemology for yourself" (survey respondent, 2013).

Another person implied that the university is not a welcoming place: "At our institution the word is that tenure track professors are 'weeded out' at the point of rehiring after the 3 year initial contract (prior to being able to apply for tenure). To that end the push to perform is immediate and intense" (survey respondent, 2013).

Another respondent mentioned that the tenure and promotion process is unclear and largely determined by the personal whim of those with power: "The requirements for tenure are vague. The target changes dependent on the promotion and tenure committee. As well the vice-president academic has the final say and it does not matter what the p&t committee recommend" (survey respondent, 2013). Vagueness most likely fuels fear.

There was no difference between the answers of those at research-intensive and teaching universities. Both sets of respondents, eight of which were at research-intensive universities and three at teaching universities, acknowledged that performativity was at their institutions and all worked strategically to address performance expectations. Neoliberalism and performativity appear to influence varied institutions similarly. Perhaps this is because neoliberalism focuses on competition for students at the local, national, and even international levels at varied institutional types through means such as institutional rankings. These rankings include criteria on professors' work.

Findings for Tenured Professors

Four of the tenured professors were at research-intensive universities, and one was at a teaching university. All five tenured professors agreed with untenured professors that performativity exists at their universities. Further, tenured professors also felt performativity had been at universities for a while. It had been in place since they started working there. However, the majority of tenured professors (three out of five), unlike untenured, stated they didn't engage in specific strategies with the aim of adding them to their curriculum vitae. This is most likely due to their greater sense of job security as they are tenured. Like untenured professors, most tenured professors (four out of five) felt that fear was present at universities. But, unlike untenured faculty, four of the five tenured professors felt that their institutions mentored younger faculty. This is an interesting finding: Why do perceptions about mentorship differ? It could be due to the random nature of the replies, that is, that untenured professors who replied to the study come from institutions that have (or are perceived to have) little mentorship, while the tenured faculty were the opposite. Alternatively, there may be a gap in perceptions, with tenured professors feeling that they provide guidance, and younger faculty not recognizing it as such, or perhaps the mentorship that is given doesn't meet the needs of newer faculty.

Finally, tenured professors provided a number of insights into performativity, focused around issues with tenure and promotion in their comments:

> The tenure and promotion process is scary for new faculty at my university. When I came to this research-intensive university, I applied for early tenure since I had worked at other universities prior to this one but had never applied for tenure and promotion. The process was not scary for me as I went in with a lot of publications, teaching awards, and outstanding service recognition. It was not, however, a slam dunk since some T and P members had obviously not read my tenure package as evidenced by their comments in my decision letter which pointed out incorrect information or commented on my promotion to Associate Professor (even though I was hired at that rank and therefore was only requesting tenure). It was a humbling experience and caused me to volunteer to sit on the T and P committee as soon as I was eligible. Since then, I have mentored nine faculty members through either tenure or promotion or both. I have tried to teach them the tricks to get past members who say comments like: "I had to wait five years to be promoted so everyone else should" or "She only published in 30 different journals so we do not really see breadth". Conversely, I have read packages where a person is pushed through because of ethnicity even though the person only had two or three publications and served on one or two small committees. We do not have standard requirements for tenure or promotion at an institutional level and at the department level, it is not followed in my discipline. (survey respondent, 2013)

> I have seen performativity increase during my 16 years as a faculty member. Faculty are also compensated through applications for merit that are adjudicated by a faculty voted onto an adjudication committee. I have deliberately decided to boycott the process – I do not apply and I will not review applications. (survey respondent, 2013)

> From an institutional perspective, I think some system of rewards/penalties to encourage, promote and support faculty research, quality teaching, and participation in the governance of the institution. For many faculty, I know this results in feelings of being pressured and that it may promote fear and insecurity in some. For myself, I have always felt that the work I WANTED to do was the work my department and university should value, so I have always felt that I was doing as I wished and being rewarded for doing so. Very early in my career, however, (and outside of Canada) I worked in a rather high pressure research centre

funded by soft money and it was very clear then that getting contracts and writing timely reports were a necessity for keeping one's job. I did not feel fear or personal insecurity in this situation, but I felt pressured to work excessive hours (80–90 hrs/wk) and I worried for colleagues who might not "make the grade." (survey respondent, 2013)

Our university has a yearly evaluation process associated with merit pay. It is a useful process to help new faculty determine if they are on track to receive tenure. While I think most people worry about attaining tenure, there should be no surprise if they have received satisfactory scores. If scores are not satisfactory, there is mentoring in place. (survey respondent, 2013)

CONCLUSIONS AND RECOMMENDATIONS

Currently, neoliberalism is the main discourse in many of the economic and educational facets of Western societies. This rhetoric privileges the market and economic profitability through means such as customer choice, performance standards and targets, budgets and statistical comparison, and goal setting and benchmarking. Drawing on Lyotard and Foucault, Ball has theorized this system as performativity. The focus on profitability is affecting actions and behaviors at the institutional and personnel levels. For example, within the context of postsecondary institutions, many professors in Faculties of Education are forced to engage in specific outcome-based behaviors to meet performance targets. At the university level, the tenure and promotion process is the clearest example of major performance targets that influence behavior.

A review of tenure and promotion over the century demonstrates that the process has always been nebulous and subject to administrator power. Over the century, faculty association pressure has led to the establishment of more procedural steps and committee involvement but the process remains ill-defined. This lack of clarity tends to foster performative actions, as individuals do what they can with the aim of meeting unclear but essential career targets. Despite the existing limitations, the research study described above supports this assertion. It found that performativity is indeed found in Canadian universities and that untenured professors are strategically working to meet tenure and promotion expectations through performative actions such as recycling papers, pushing for grants that they don't really need for their work, and getting good teaching scores. These professors do not feel mentored by their universities, and a small majority do feel fear. In comparison, tenured professors state they are less strategic in their actions and feel that they mentor younger faculty. They agree that performativity exists and state that it has been in the faculty for some time. Both groups commented on problems with the tenure and promotion system as a major driver of performativity.

Thus, one of the major dangers of neoliberalism is that it can foster inauthentic actions on the part of assistant professors who aim to keep their jobs. This can affect professors' identities as they may feel a disconnect between what they are expected to do and what they would like to do. For example, they may cut their service work down as it is given limited importance in the tenure and promotion process, or they may attempt to engage in strategic actions that increase their publications, such as publishing their graduate students' work with their names attached to it, rather than doing the work and activities they would really like to do.

Recommendations for addressing the results of the research on performativity in North American universities are presented next. They are divided into two sections: recommendations within and outside of today's major discourse.

Within the Current Discourse

1. Clarity and Transparency

The historical overview included above shows that tenure and promotion criteria have been and remain nebulous, despite the effort of faculty associations. Further, the comments of surveyed faculty highlight a number of issues with tenure and promotion including unclear criteria and favoritism. Neoliberalism includes within its doctrine the concept of transparency – that criteria should be openly presented so that individuals can make their choices. Thus, it is only being consistent with neoliberalism to ensure that tenure and promotion criteria are clearly delineated in quantifiable terms, such as the number of publications that an individual must have. As well, the tenure and promotion committee should be open to the person being evaluated. He or she should be able to hear what is said about himself or herself and have a chance to respond.

2. Mentorship

The survey illustrated gaps in the views of tenured versus untenured professors regarding mentorship in their faculties. Untenured faculty do not feel mentored by their more senior colleagues. Mentorship of untenured faculty should consider their needs. Martinez (2008) reviews literature arguing that teacher educators face a number of challenges when they enter universities and that university research is stressful. These are related to the unique conditions of teacher educators in contrast to the work of professors in other disciplines. Martinez recommends identification and recognition of the unique challenges faced by teacher educators and the development of a good induction program that includes details specific to the position and the ability to engage in cross-disciplinary work.

3. Appropriate Criteria

Like Martinez (2008), Murray (2012) argues that teacher educators have difficult and different work than that of other university professors as they straddle two worlds with varying criteria: the world of academia and the world of schools, both of which have their own standards and policies. Further, education professors have to spend time building relationships. These conditions, in addition to the complexity and subtlety of their pedagogy, are not considered in the quantified rating scales used to assess them. To be both fair and valid, these factors should be considered, as well as other relevant elements in performative assessment criteria. Education professors could actually be involved in selecting and developing the criteria that will be used to assess them. This would be respectful of their professionalism and would help them to maintain authentic identities as they focus on work that is of value to them.

Alternative Discourse Possibilities to Performativity

Lyotard and other postmodern writers have exploded the myth of the meta-narrative or discourse that structures meaning. We, thus, have the possibility of refusing to buy into the market-based neoliberal discourse and embracing other more humane discourses. We can recognize that a business ideology does not "fit" educational settings and find a more appropriate one, such as the UK's previous professional model, which believes in the potential of individuals to do quality work when entrusted with it. We can recognize that professors and teachers are not "average" employees and tend to be highly self-motivated. We can embrace the potential of empowerment and care to succeed. Meng (2009) argues that the current discourse damages teachers' identities and squashes creative thought. The author suggests that we take on the postmodern qualities of play to openly and joyfully explore alternative possibilities and embrace non-performative goals. We can change our metaphor to be teachers as artists and designers, not unmotivated factory workers.

Similarly, Johnson (2005) argues that performative measures are incomplete and political: They are chosen by particular individuals with power who have their own agendas, and often this criteria fails to consider some of the most significant educational goals, such as how much critical thinking is included in classes. The data that are collected can also be manipulated. Johnson argues that we should consider what aims are most important and maintain a sense of humor about the current ideology as we, laughingly, explore its limitations and alternatives.

Individual Actions

The two previous sections explored what can be done at the institutional level to address issues related to performativity. As mentioned, performativity affects actions, and is best illustrated in the tenure and promotion process. It can lead tenure-track professors to engage in performative actions such as recycling papers or inflating grades. As a result, some professors can lose connection with themselves, can become inauthentic, and thus negatively affect their personal and professional identities. Individual professors can work to maintain their authenticity through continuing to believe and find meaning and validation in the work they do, and through doing work that they value. They can continue to love their discipline and remember or foster what first drew them to the field (Palmer, 1998).

They can also think holistically about their work by connecting service with teaching and scholarship and link in to the needs and interests of their local and global educational communities. Focusing on work they value in partnership with these communities provides opportunities for professors to provide leadership and insights, for them to be public intellectuals. In the words of Freire (1998), "When we live our lives with the authenticity demanded by the practice of teaching that is also learning and learning that is also teaching, we are participating in a total experience... In this experience the beautiful, the decent, and the serious form a circle with hands joined" (pp. 31–32).

CHAPTER FOUR

Living and Working in a Global Space

Liminality Within an Academic Life

SUSAN CRICHTON

BACKGROUND

I start writing this chapter after visiting Mandela's cell on Robben Island, Cape Town, South Africa. For almost as long as my professional career, Nelson Mandela was held in prison. At the age of 72, he was finally released and resumed his work to build a better and more humane version of his county – eventually becoming the first president of a new South Africa. At the age of 80, he retired and resumed his activist work, focusing on issues of social justice and human dignity.

One might ask, why start a chapter acknowledging a man of such stature? My reply: When academics are offered the privileges and freedoms inherent in what constitutes our work, how do we make our work matter in significant ways? I start writing this chapter in Africa, as the continent pauses to consider a world without Mandela's watchful gaze. It feels increasingly important to mindfully ponder what might count in an academic life, and how our efforts might actually be counted and accounted for – especially when weighed against such selfless commitments as those made by Mandela and others.

Cameron (1963) states, "not everything that can be counted counts, and not everything that counts can be counted." While this quote is often misattributed to Einstein, the importance of the words rest in the messiness of valuing what is truly important work, specifically for this chapter written within an academy driven by the pursuit of research excellence typically evidenced in tenure and promotion of its faculty members. Annually, highly rated global academic institutions wrestle to benefit from metrics by which they rank themselves (TSL Education, 2012), seemingly against a growing tide of educational options and critiques questioning the relevance and value of higher education (Menand, 2011). As an educator who joined the academy at age 50, I naively took the stance that meaningful, good work (Räsänen, 2008; Shulman, 2005) would lead to merit, promotion, and tenure. This chapter describes my experience, which has resulted in tenure at two research-intensive institutions and a visiting professorship at a third. I illustrate this academic trek with two personally "worthy" projects.

Informed by educators such as Sir John Daniel (2010), this chapter muses on ways in which academics can democratically and proactively participate in mindful, contextually relevant educational activities that are essential for our increasingly globalized and challenged twenty-first-century learning needs to inform authentic, relevant learning (Thomas & Brown, 2011; Trilling & Fadel, 2009). Daniel (2010) reminds us that any meaningful educational reform must "lead to the nurturing of human capabilities that allow [students] the freedoms to lead worthwhile lives. It should not merely train individuals to become the human capital required for economic production" (p. 6).

In this chapter, I position scholarship and academic work within challenging contexts (Crichton, 2013; Crichton & Onguko, 2013) and use that term, inclusively, to recognize the varying degrees to which individuals struggle globally with circumstances, conditions, or environmental constraints that afford little or no access to fundamental needs. These include access to available and affordable electricity; reliable, unfiltered, or uncensored Internet; formal learning and/or opportunities for ongoing formal learning that support individual learning needs; participation in learning activities potentially restricted by cultural or religious beliefs; clean water and adequate sanitation; fair and just leadership; adequate nutrition and safe food supply; a safe environment free from hostilities and violence; support for the disabled; and adequate financial support to fund basics such as health care, school fees, appropriate clothing, and other needs.

Mandela (2005) continually told audiences, "Overcoming poverty is not a gesture of charity. It is an act of justice. It is a protection of a fundamental human right, the right to dignity and a decent life." I would suggest academics, within the academy, have a significant role to play to ensure and protect those rights, locally and internationally. Drawing on two projects rooted in social justice, I will share the institutional response to each and the impact they had on my own practice.

To conclude the chapter, I will discuss the liminality of living and working globally while maintaining an increasingly blurred professional and personal local presence. I will explore how one is ever the outsider in a global setting while gradually becoming an outsider locally through the development of an ever-expanding worldview and time away from home, campus, and community.

A PICTURE IS WORTH A THOUSAND MEALS — ONE MOMENT AMONG A PROJECT

Less than two years into my first academic appointment, at a time when my contemporaries were purposefully applying for significant grants and writing for top-tier journals, I eagerly joined a five-year CIDA (Canadian International Development Agency) project, located in western China and jointly implemented by three Canadian universities and a provincial ministry of education (Agriteam, 2013). The project goals were to improve basic education (grades 1–9) in regions of western China, especially in locations where issues of minority and gender equality were problematic. Underpinning the project was the need to design a distance education approach at a time when satellite options were new, mobile technologies were vague sketches in designers' notebooks, and instructional design and media development were in the hands of government production houses. Months into implementing the project, we were able to offer professional learning opportunities in rural and remote areas and begin to co-create local content, illustrated with regional images and culturally sensitive examples. This approach was a significant change to existing practice as training and content development traditionally were offered and developed in government centers located in large urban centers. I've written extensively about this elsewhere (Crichton, 2012) and include a brief account here:

> During a school visit in a spectacular mountainous region in rural western Sichuan province, I wandered into the central playground area. People in this region tend to be poor as the area is challenging to farm and many are Tibetan, a minority group in China…. It was lunchtime, and the children had left their [unheated, cement block] classrooms to enjoy the sunshine…. We all were basking in the warmth like a collection of cats, when I decided to film the children as they enjoyed their lunches and chatted happily on chairs surrounding the play area. I had time to spend as a group of graduate students and their supervisor, who had travelled with us from Beijing, were conducting interviews with community members concerning the impact of poverty on schooling and regional development. Sitting back down, I scrolled through the pictures I had just taken, ensuring that I had what I wanted when I noticed a group of children in one image who were sitting just on the margins of one the photo – these children were just outside the… [centre of the] frame, but it was something about the freeze frame of the photograph that allowed me to notice something that I had not been able to observe when I watched the children earlier.

> I showed the picture to my colleague who, fortunately for me, spoke enough English as I spoke no Chinese. In wonderfully descriptive yet thoughtfully selected English she explained, "Those children are pretending to eat lunch. Those children are too poor to bring food from home." Literally they were the children in the margins of more than my photograph. They were ones who typically formed the large numbers of minority children who dropped out of rural schools after their compulsory Basic Education (grades 1–9) was

completed – if not earlier. In an odd drama, these children sat off to the side, with their empty lunch boxes, pretending to eat, taking the same amount of time and effort as their classmates with actual food.

Ironically, immediately after this observation, we were taken to lunch; a meal in nearby hotel. While nothing fancy, the fact that it was warm and nourishing immediately took away the chill of the cold morning in the unheated school.

Needless to say, the topic of children pretending to eat lunch dominated our conversation. Through my translator I asked about subsidized lunch programs, explaining the role they played in many North American schools. The principal of the school was quite interested, both in the fact that Canadian schools needed food programs, but also in the mechanics of these programs – whose responsibility it was, who paid, how were they managed, etc. Our consensus was that it was wrong for children to drop out of school because they were hungry, but the professor, an expert in educational policy, noted there was nothing in school fees or government policy that allowed for lunch programs. It was then that the Lunch for Learning idea was born. I asked the principal if there was anything wrong with a grass roots initiative to start a lunch program. I proposed asking the Canadian experts to contribute small amounts of money to the program, donating left over Chinese currency or making periodic contributions. I explained that grass roots projects NEVER paid overhead or administrative costs, but local people should be paid to make and distribute simple hot lunches each school day. We discussed the plan for the next two days, and when I left, I gave the principal all the foreign cash I had (about $150 CDN) and 300 RMB (about $40). This was enough to start the program and feed the students for the first few months.

Over the next year, project administrators, both Canadian and Chinese, regularly sent money out to the principal. As expected, Canadian consultants donated rather than converted their remaining RMB, and the lunch program grew. Eventually, almost a year to the day it started, the principal emailed me (via the original interpreter) that I no longer needed to send money, the teachers at the school had taken over the program as they felt they needed to be the ones responsible.

THE LONG LEGS OF KIND ACTS

During the next year of the project I forgot about Lunch for Learning. However, near the end of the work, I attended a meeting with a Chinese expert on educational policy, and, of course, it was the professor from the Sichuan trip. This man had the ear of government, and when he saw me again, he explained how much the trip to Sichuan had impacted him. Further, he explained that he had put the issue of lunch programs on the agenda for government meetings, encouraging that it be entrenched in policy and the images became part of his research reports and findings – something very new within the Ministry of Education (Crichton, 2012).

It is hard to quantify the impact that small intervention within the larger project had on the participants – both Canadian and Chinese. China, especially western China, was considered a challenging context at the time of our project. Our work took place before the Olympics, China's manned space flight, and its emergence as a global economic power. We wrestled with power shortages and lack of Internet connectivity, and we tried to do the right thing by creating content in local languages (Uighur and Tibetan) and showcasing minority culture in illustrations and examples. After the project, most of us went back to our "regular" work. I doubt Lunch for Learning had raised even $1,000. I had gained some expertise/reputation as a distance educator, content developer, and international development worker, and I kept in touch with many of my Chinese colleagues for years. Four years of work in China (some online and some in country) translated into service and international work on my professional CV and tenure application.

Eventually, several academics on the project were able to negotiate with administrators for the opportunity to write a few anecdotal, rather than data-informed, articles about the project experiences, such as the one cited above. One team member used the project as the site for his master's thesis. While my work on the project had not counted for much in terms of institutionally recognized research/scholarship, I do know that at one time my picture of those children had found its way to the Ministry of Education at the People's Republic of China where it might have helped inform a bit of policy, and the importance of digital documentation as provocation for action and reflection is increasingly an essential aspect of my work.

ADDING THE X TO STEM

In 2009 STEM, the integration of Science, Technology, Engineering, and Mathematics, was relatively a new idea. Imperial Oil, a significant funder within our community, had provided a grant opportunity titled *Inspiring Careers in STEM* with criteria including the following:

- An academic partnership between the Faculties of Education and Engineering
- A maximum duration of two years
- A budget less than $50,000

Accepted projects were later asked to reduce their budgets to be under $25,000 so additional projects could be funded.

Building on my experiences in western China described in the previous section, I was already exploring the potential of simple, appropriate technologies to support learning in challenging contexts. I had gone so far as to work with hardware developers to design a simple tablet device two years before the release of the first iPad. The experience with satellite dishes in China at time a when portable, personal DVD players were becoming common had caused me to question the appropriateness of lab-based technologies for student use, partially because of the exceedingly expensive infrastructure required to support them.

Technologies (Conteh, 2003) are deemed appropriate when they satisfy a number of conditions including the following:

- Being compatible with local, cultural, and economic conditions (i.e., the human, material, and cultural resources of the economy)
- Utilizing locally available material and energy resources
- Requiring tools and processes maintained and operationally controlled by the local population

Conteh's definition draws from Schumacher's (1973) recommendation that technology should be compatible with the level of sophistication of the society in which it is applied and hence should disrupt that society the least. In other words, it should fit a context and address a specific challenge. Believing this, I proposed a partnership with Dr. Dave Irvine-Halliday, the founder of Light Up The World Foundation (www.lutw.org) and winner of a Rolex Award for Enterprise. Irvine-Halliday had developed an LED lighting solution that was changing the quality of daily life for individuals in some of the most rural and remote regions of the world. By replacing kerosene lamps, his simple, small-scale solar-powered systems were improving the air quality of homes, creating cost savings, and helping children do homework in the evening without damaging their eyesight.

We designed our STEM project for grade 5/6 classes in a local elementary school walking distance from the university. We situated the project at that grade level knowing it is a time when some children begin to shy away from math and science, therefore limiting their chances to pursue careers in STEM-related disciplines. Our project objectives included (1) helping teachers forge strong curricular links within the existing Science, ICT, Math, and Social Studies programs; (2) establishing a stronger partnership between the university faculties and their neighboring school; (3) fostering rich links between the engineering students and the school; (4) establishing good habits of the mind concerning social justice, global citizenship, critical thinking, spatial literacy, math, science, and technology; and (5) suggesting that by situating the projects in social justice and humanitarian thinking, we could encourage girls to consider careers in STEM-related fields.

We imagined the engineering students would work with the students and their teachers to (1) identify challenges facing children, families, and their schools and communities in the developing world and (2) use design thinking to work collaboratively to imagine and build workable solutions. We felt that once the challenges/issues had been identified, teams consisting of both student groups would (1) research/design an appropriate technology solution to address a particular challenge; (2) explore geographic/contextual issues; (3) sketch their projects; (4) build a prototype model; and (5) share their solutions with their friends and families at an open house. We offered two examples of appropriate technologies developed in their community: Light Up The World (www.lutw.org) and CAWST (www.cawst.org), the developer of the biosand water filter.

As the students began their work, the horrific 2010 earthquake in Haiti happened. The children were bombarded with news reports of the damage, deaths, and injuries. We used this catastrophic event as a purpose for their projects, believing that by designing solutions to the challenges they were seeing in the media it would help the students to understand the positive impact of the humanitarian efforts that were taking place. The design challenge for each group was to design and prototype a solution to a challenge someone their age would be facing in Haiti as a result of the earthquake.

The first year of our project was deemed a success, and the students' solutions to the design challenges were complex and inspiring. Two doctoral students were involved, and one used the project as the site for her research. The engineering students gained benefit as their participation counted toward completion of their program's community outreach requirement. The school was pleased, and the open house was a success. The deans from both faculties attended, as did more than 200 community and family members.

Reflecting on the successes and challenges of the first year of the project, we decided to reconceptualize it slightly and maximize the opportunity to support the implementation of an appropriate technology in a challenging context. One of the doctoral students was returning to rural western Kenya to do his data collection. His site was quite a challenging context – there was no Internet connectivity, limited mobile phone access, and one of the students in the local school had recently died from waterborne disease. By using the doctoral student's access to the community and his understanding of the context and language, the students in Canada could become the project managers for the installation of a CAWST biosand water filter. They could also collaborate with the Kenyan students on a domestic water quality study, using the connectivity provided through the doctoral student's mobile phone. Everyone was thrilled. We recast the project and sought permission to revise the budget to include the expenditure of $800 for the water filter implementation and community training. Volunteers from the Canadian CAWST offices were prepared to come to the project school, and the revised budget would allow a CAWST trainer, who was already in Kenya, to train the local community and school on the maintenance and use of the filter once it was in place.

Then the project stalled. The administrative committee managing the Imperial Oil STEM grant at the university reviewed our project modification and rejected our request. The committee was made up of academic colleagues from both faculties. The request was denied on two grounds: (1) appropriate technologies were questioned as legitimate technologies and (2) once budgets are approved, the committee felt they should not be modified. I was stunned, and I realized that we had gone too far, without permission, to turn back over $800. My husband and I discussed the situation and agreed that if I could not find another solution, we would simply have to pay for the water filter and training ourselves. I re-submitted my budget modification to the committee four times. Finally, the chair came to my office and stated that the committee's hands were tied. The conditions for the grant did not offer them any direction, and she suggested I ask my dean for advice.

Fortunately, the dean had participated in the project open house and knew the students' commitment to the work. When I explained the reason for the changes to the budget, he initially supported the committee's response, stating major grants typically did not allow flexibility in budget modification, regardless of the reason. We were at a standstill. I do not recall all the particulars of how we moved on; I think I suggested I would just pay for it myself and return the $800 to Imperial Oil, or it might have been the story of the girl dying from dirty water we could purify, but I left the office with permission to modify the budget.

The water filter still functions in the school, the villagers have raised funds for a few community filters, the project informed a portion of the doctoral student's dissertation (Onguko, 2010), and students and their teachers in two different schools and worlds apart became partners in the improvement of water quality in both locations. By adapting our STEM work to consider human-centered design based on authentic need, we unintentionally added our version of the "x" to STEMx by introducing design thinking and its emphasis on empathy (Stanford University Institute of Design, 2013). Internationally, STEM projects are now being encouraged to become STEMx or STEAM projects, recognizing the importance of the arts and humanities in the project design process (Sousa & Pilecki, 2013). Design thinking continues to influence my work, helping me to continually question who benefits from the projects I engage in and what the value might be to all the partners. If our research participants and project partners are not at the center of the work, then truly, why are we doing it in the first place and what is its purpose?

ACADEMIA OR CONSULTING: HAVE YOU CONSIDERED CHANGING YOUR JOB?

This chapter has caused me to pause and consider the university as a contested site and the conflicting messages academics receive concerning what constitutes service and what constitutes intellectual activity. I still hold tightly to my initial, and somewhat naive, stance that an academic life can be one devoted to the cause of social justice. I recognize the privilege I have been afforded by coming to the academy after a rich and often challenging career in K–12 education. I continue to relish each opportunity, and I am learning to subject them to a heightened scrutiny of impact, challenge, and potential value. Since the first opportunity in China, I have been fortunate to work with colleagues around the globe, from East Africa to Bhutan, China to Chile. I have established a line of research focusing on learning innovation, appropriate technology, and design thinking.

However, since coming to the academy in 2001, I have observed an increasing focus on research intensity, aligned ever more closely to global metrics that judge the performance of

> world class universities across all of their core missions – teaching, research, knowledge transfer and international outlook. The top universities rankings employ 13 carefully calibrated performance indicators to provide the most comprehensive and balanced comparisons available, which are trusted by students, academics, university leaders, industry and governments. (TSL Education, 2012)

Recently, in a conversation with a senior colleague, the issue of work that counts and work that is counted by the university arose. We discussed the need to obtain grants and to publish in top-tier journals, many of which are not open access or open source and therefore are unavailable to most of the colleagues with whom I write. Often, the cost of the publications makes access to the content prohibitive and yet, increasingly universities are applying the same metrics for publication in these journals as well to achieve academically rigorous track records that help secure international funding. When I expressed my frustration with these metrics and benchmarks, my colleague suggested maybe I should just leave the academy and go into consulting, suggesting my values might be in conflict with those of the university. This comment has stayed with me for almost a year. It was not offered in a mean-spirited way; it was rather matter of fact, almost a statement of the obvious.

And it is this statement that takes me back to the opening of this chapter. Ironically, as I finish writing this, the news of Mandela's death hangs in the air – his life an example of what can be when one dedicates oneself to doing good and forgiveness. What would Mandela have thought about the G15 metrics and the increasing focus on world rankings as the measure of a top-tier university? His often cited belief "Education is the most powerful weapon which you can use to change the world" (Makoni & MacGregor, 2013) risks being affected by the current climate that privileges first or single authorship in top-tier publications and success in obtaining well-recognized grants, that allow for university overhead fees. Determining what to value and what counts is messy business, and enacting it when working with colleagues in challenging, global contexts only confounds this difficulty.

LIMINALITY: NAVIGATING THE SPACES BETWEEN, CONTINUOUSLY

During the first project described in this chapter, I cumulatively spent more than a year of the five-year project on the ground in Beijing and sites in western China. Since 2008, I have worked with colleagues in East Africa 10 times, Pakistan once, and returned to Bhutan for a second time. I do not take these opportunities for granted, and I accept each with a high degree of humility and gratitude. However, each adds a dimension of what I had previously called complexity to my sense of place and what actually matters at home. Recently, a valued colleague introduced me to the notion of liminality, a concept from which I am gaining comfort.

Turner (1987) describes liminality as a period of transition betwixt and between states – a *rite de passage* between three identifiable phases. The first phase, separation, suggests a detachment from an existing state. The second phase, limen, is an ambiguous state between the phases. The third phase is aggregation, which is seen as the consummation or completion of the transition. While it is all too tidy to try to represent actual life experiences into linear, discretely identifiable categories, Turner explains liminality deals with the unstructured aspects of lives, noting that "life is punctuated by critical moments of transitions" (p. 5) and can be evidenced/affected by newly achieved status or rank within an ever-changing social structure. Bettis and Mills (2006) position liminality within the academic community, suggesting those in a liminal space experience within the academy "structure invisibility" evidenced in a general sense of anxiety, uncertainty over what work is valued, and worries about their cohesion with program/unit and its impact on faculty evaluation (p. 67). Bettis and Mills identify 12 categories that contribute to a sense of liminality within an academic life, and I would suggest that these are universal, to varying degrees, for academics around the world. However, what makes liminality even more curious is when it is experienced across multiple locations.

This curiosity/complexity aligns with the anthropological act of making the familiar strange and the strange familiar (Spiro, 1990). Citing Lévi-Strauss, Spiro suggests being betwixt and between rarely allow us to be on neutral terms with our own social group (p. 58). The act of transitioning between the two, the familiar and the strange, allows us "to come to view the familiar with a greater degree of objectivity than would otherwise be the case" (p. 48). Further, one might suggest that while we do not end up fully understanding either, we might end up knowing enough to question both and act with a different sense of agency than colleagues from one or the other contexts. I recognize my growing comfort with liminal spaces has put tension on family, friends, and colleagues. This neutrality is played out in a wardrobe that is increasingly suited to an African climate and norms, a heightened frustration of administrative practices that feel like they micro-manage academic life, and an increasing intolerance for seemingly petty concerns that do not even begin to address larger issues of social justice facing those living in challenging contexts here and abroad.

It is within this rich liminal space I believe we academics can be charged to do our best work. Our place of privilege as public intellectuals and educational leaders requires us to ensure that work that counts is counted and respected within the academy. Those of us with tenure must help colleagues and administrators to translate the metrics as written into metrics that can be lived in what Mandela would have called "acts of justice." My naive but delightful time within the academy suggests it can be done. Not through enormous, showy actions, but rather through simple, everyday intentions such as photography that depicts poverty or asking yet another time for changes to budget criteria, pushing boundaries and questioning established practices. Collaborating with graduate students, allowing junior colleagues to be principal investigators, publishing in open-source journals, and writing grants that allow faculty exchanges across institutions are simple steps of awareness. They are strangely familiar, and I would suggest they are the right things to do to make an academic life count in an increasingly global and challenging world.

CHAPTER FIVE

Performativity in the Academy

Negotiating Ambition, Desire, and the Demands of Femininity[1]

LYNN BOSETTI AND SABRE CHERKOWSKI

I think the main cost [of my professional ambitions] was that my husband of twenty plus years decided that he didn't like the person that I'd become because it's really a transformation that I was going through. And the caretaking role, the executive function that I'd had within our family essentially I was now using in other sectors. I was using it in the family too, but he actually didn't feel that that was okay and he left our family... it was hard for me to not beat myself up about that. Had I actually become a person that was unlovable by being in this job? And to some extent I think I internalized the fact that that was probably true. Maybe I was. (Patti)

This story is familiar to many academic women with ambition to achieve in their professional lives while balancing the multiple entanglements of femininity, desire, and family life. There is an inherent loneliness in negotiating this chosen life path with little access to the personal or private dimensions of the lives of fellow travelers of how life might be otherwise. It may be a divided life is endemic to being a working professional regardless of gender; however, the desire for integration, wholeness, and congruity between our interior and outer lives, between our professional and personal identity, resonates in the narratives of many academic women and in the choices they make regarding how to live their lives.

The organizational cultures of professional faculties such as education and nursing are regulated by an inherited implicit social structure that has shaped the field and professional identity of professors (Acker & Dillabough, 2007). This is particularly problematic for academic women who are positioned within this double entanglement of balancing the demands of femininity (mother, wife, daughter, sister) with those of intellectual life (Marso, 2006). In an institutional culture that lacks rules or mechanisms to shepherd faculty through this process of identity formation, individuals can feel anxious, confused, or incompetent as they negotiate the contradictions in their personal and professional lives and deal with issues of power, resistance, and the demands of performativity (Acker & Dillabough, 2007; Blackmore, 2002; Bosetti, Kawalilak, & Patterson, 2008).

The intent of this study was to identify and describe the interacting and competing factors that influence and affect the entanglement experienced by academic women within the confines of their professional and personal lives. These women share their desire for freedom and enhanced possibilities. By documenting and providing the stories of their struggle to negotiate the demands of femininity and academic life we are contributing to what Rosi Bradotti (1994) calls a *feminist genealogy*. Genealogies are politically formed counter-memories that keep us connected to the experiences and speaking voices of women with recognition of our inheritance from our feminist mothers and sisters (p. 207). By reading the women's accounts sympathetically it helps us to interpret our dilemmas as a shared effort to articulate and act on desires.

We used narrative inquiry to access and present the stories of our participants. The women in this study, professors in Faculties of Education in Canada, have invested substantial time in the formal education system as students, practicing teachers, and graduate students. Through this socialization they have learned the lessons of dutiful academic daughters reciting their intellectual fathers/ grandfathers – the theorists who frame their profession (e.g., Dewey, Kohlberg, Hegel, Marx, Freire, Weber, etc.) and find themselves constrained by narratives not always of their choosing. Hélène Cixous (1981) explains, "The moment [academic] women open their mouths – women more often than men – they are immediately asked whose name and from what theoretical standpoint they are speaking, who is their master and where they are coming from: they have, in short to salute… and to show their identity papers"(cited in Luke & Gore, 1992, p. 4). To be successful they adopted these discourses to frame their dissertations and get published in journals. They learned to be high achievers to gain praise and recognition. The system of academic apprenticeship, of gaining credential knowledge and a certified identity, has an impact on their life pathways, and formation of their identity.

Through sharing the experiences of these women and the consequences of their decision we hope to provide deeper insight into particular pathways to being successful academics and to create the space to contemplate how it might be otherwise. Women have always told stories to one another, although they have not always shared their stories publicly (Heilbrun, 1988). Adrienne Rich (1976) writes, "it is only the willingness of women to share the 'private and often painful experience' that will enable them to achieve a true description of the work and to free and encourage one another" to steady the course or choose alternative pathways to fulfillment (cited in Heilbrun, 1988, p. 69).

Through this research we join together to contest the social interpretations of our existence as academic women, to make sense of our dilemmas in a shared effort to articulate and act on desires, opening alternative pathways to what it means to be a successful academic woman.

NARRATIVE INQUIRY AND LIMINALITY

There is a solid body of research on the challenges for women in academia (Acker & Dillabough, 2007; Denker, 2009; Saunderson, 2002), the politics of balancing family and work (Maguire, 2008; Mason, Goulden, & Wolfinger, 2006; Pillay, 2009), and the difficulties of constructing professional identities (Archer, 2008; Clark, 2006; Lester, 2008; Pillay, 2009; Pitt & Phelan, 2008). Our research explores the implications for women academics embroiled in the multiple demands of femininity with the desire to live a more integrated life (Marso, 2006). We examine their struggle to be self-defining as they challenge the normative/ societal meaning of family, marriage, and work, and in so doing, experience society's disdain as they attempt to live within the confines of dominant narratives of what it means to be a good mother/wife/academic. Popular and journalistic culture of postfeminist times often portray contemporary career-oriented women as burned-out, infertile, and suffering from a man shortage, demonstrating that what we were promised by feminism is impossible – we cannot have it all. The stories in this study accentuate the challenges and difficulties of attempting to live a full life in both personal and professional spheres, and bring into question the pathways to and the meaning of being a successful academic woman. Through these stories we can be more conscious of the choices before us.

Narrative Inquiry

Narrative is an intimate aspect of our lives, one of the ways through which we describe, share, and come to understand our experiences in the world (Clandinin & Connelly, 1994, Connelly & Clandinin, 1996; Eisner & Peshkin, 1990; Richardson, 2000). Baldwin (2005) explains:

> We make our lives bigger or smaller, more expansive or more limited, according the interpretation of life that is our story. Whether we speak or write these stories, we constantly weave life events into narrative and interpret everything that happens through the veil of story. (p. ix)

Engaging in narrative inquiry can lead to altering existing beliefs, attitudes, and mindsets as the participants and the researchers question and challenge their stories of theory and practice (Richardson, 2000). Since both the reader and the writer are actively engaged in a mutual process of sense making, the narrative as process and text becomes a lived phenomenon, constantly changing with each storyteller, each reader, and with each draft of the writing (Baldwin, 2005; Connelly & Clandinin, 1996). In this way, this text can become a vehicle for re-storying the culture of academia, with its legacy of power and isolation, to a culture of community, negotiation, and agency.

In the prevailing corporate culture of many Canadian universities the focus is on tasks, structures, procedures, and outcomes driven by a research-intensive agenda (Reimer, 2004). Women academics in professional faculties are challenged with balancing increasingly intense research workloads that emphasize individual performance with the inherent expectations in professional faculties of collegiality and an emphasis on caretaking (Acker & Dillabough, 2007; Bosetti et al., 2008). The management of these workloads, institutional assumptions, and resulting identity negotiations can be problematic for women academics attempting to also balance families, meet home-life obligations, and cultivate fulfilling intimate relationships (Armenti, 2004; Saunderson, 2002; Ward & Wolf-Wendel, 2004).

Liminality

We draw on the theory of liminality to deepen our analysis of the women's stories. Victor Turner (1967) described liminality as a transitional period and status during rites of passage among individuals in African tribes. He describes this as an "inter-structural stage" in which individuals have given up one social state, but are yet to enter the new prescribed social state and so are "betwixt and between" social statues and without a fixed identity (Bettis & Mills, 2006, p. 61). Gilbert (2006) uses the Sanskrit word *Antevasin*, the one who dwells at the border, to describe such a state:

> The border dweller lives on the edge of the forest where his spiritual masters dwell. He is no longer one of the villagers anymore – not a householder with conventional life, nor is he one of those sages who lies in the unexplored woods, fully realized. He lives inside of both worlds, but looks towards the unknown. And he was a scholar. (p. 203)

For women academics struggling to achieve an integrated identity, to reconcile the social demands and responsibilities of being a mother, partner, and academic, they can find themselves unable to live fully in any one role. The anthropological theory of liminality has since been used in a sociological capacity to understand inner conflict for social work students (Hurlock, Barlow, Phelan, Myrick, Sawa, & Rogers, 2008), in an organizational capacity to explore faculty members' understanding of their new professional identity in a restructured department (Bettis & Mills, 2006), and as a feminist perspective for understanding women's ways of being in the world (Heilbrun, 1999).

DESIGN OF STUDY

In this study we draw on the experiences of five academic women from Faculties of Education in two universities in Canada. They represent different generations and stages in academic careers. Rachel is a single, beginning professor in her late 30s, Anna and Danielle are associate professors in their early 40s with young families, Marika is a full professor in her mid-40s with children in middle school, and Patti is a mature, full professor who is divorced with grown children. Although the pathways to academia differ among these women, their common ground lies in being women, their sense-making of the shifting landscape of university culture, their struggle with the demands of femininity and academic performance, and the consequent challenge to their personal and professional/academic identity and affiliations.

We present an account of these women academics' experiences where we aim for their *voices* to speak. Respectful, attentive listening, open-mindedness, and honesty are critical to a deep dialogue experience (Belenky, McVicker Clinchy, Rule Goldberger, & Mattuck Tarule, 1986; Wheatley, 2005). We chose semi-structured dialogues and guiding themes (e.g., pathway to becoming an academic; challenges in balancing role expectations in personal and professional life; advice to other academic women) to provide space for participants to navigate the dialogue in whatever direction they needed to go. The individual dialogues were 60 to 90 minutes long, tape-recorded, and transcribed verbatim. Participants chose a pseudonym to provide the freedom and confidence to tell their story. As researchers we independently reviewed and analyzed tapes post-dialogue identifying themes, images, and metaphors. We then shared our individual thematic analyses and interpretations to determine common perspectives, diverse interpretations, and consistencies. This study is limited by the small sample size, gender specificity, and location within particular institutions. Although we do not explicitly share our stories as women academics in this study, we are complicit in our role as researchers in listening, asking questions, and analyzing the data, and have an influence on the accounts shared here.

HEARING THEIR VOICES: LISTENING TO OUR STORIES

Through sympathetically listening to these women speak their private stories we may hear our own story, a common story of what it means to be an academic. For most working professionals our struggles, anxiety, resistance, and personal compromises remain in our private life, not readily shared with colleagues. In their professional lives, these women show up as competent, achieving women who appear to be able to do it all, despite the un-sustainability of living a fragmented life where tasks and functions in other areas of their lives are tightly managed to create space for their work. We hear moments of resistance to workload, committee work, and travel to conferences that take them away for long periods of time; however, for the most part they are reluctant to use the demands of being a mother, having to accommodate their partner's work, and the need for family time or, worse yet, personal time as justifications for how they manage their work. By making compromises in their private life – such as delaying or foregoing marriage and motherhood to pursue their careers – their stories provide a limited script for being a successful female academic. The script available of the high-achieving professor is one able to manage her private and professional life in separate spheres. She appears focused, driven, and psychologically hard. Her private needs and desires are far from public view. To the external world her passion is her work; her work comprises most of her life. This is a pathway some women may choose, where success is measured in terms of output and performance.

Professional Identity

> Over the years I have observed and come to understand this unique nature of bright and driven women, at least in the academic area. We have been socialized into being independent and strong-minded. We can hold our own with either gender, and we need little from a man in terms of financial support or our identity. What we want is a partner that provides balance and compliments our energy and masculine side. It is a difficult balance because he can't be too weak, but he also has to be willing to be a partner, to let his wife shine and to support her in parenting and on the domestic front. (Marika)

As academic women in education we have invested substantial time gaining the necessary accreditations and accomplishments for realizing our academic destinies. We have become high achievers who seek validation where we often feel the most fulfilled – our intellectual life. For the women in this story, intellectual life as realized through being a professor is vital to who they are and how they flourish. When we investigate the archeology of our professional knowledge and our inheritance as academic women, our professional identity has largely been ascribed to the narrative of our intellectual fathers and grandfathers. These normative scripts (institutional inscriptions) of what it means to be a professor and do academic work have not been of our own making; as feminists we are not always able to create and inhabit feminist ways of living. While there are counter-stories from our feminist mothers and sisters, they have not penetrated the dominant culture

PERFORMATIVITY IN THE ACADEMY | 67

of the academy, but are stumbled upon by women seeking other ways to live their life as academics. Their stories reflect the challenge of aligning and integrating dispositions and traits necessary for academic success as integral to their identity and ways of being in their personal lives; however, some find these same traits are not always conducive to harmonious marriages and expectations in the realm of motherhood and wife. Patti shares her experience:

> In the evening I had trouble turning off the switch because I am always into executive function, so turning that off is hard…. My 12-year-old daughter said, "Mom you just need to stop for a minute. Just have some tea and relax." I was trying to do too many things…. I feel differently about myself when I'm doing things that have meaning and that are meaningful. It is a part of me, rather than a job I do. It's part of who I am.

The steady demand to be productive, a dominant institutional narrative, was a constant source of anxiety for these women as they strove to cultivate their professional identity while maintaining an ability to nurture passion and desire in other dimensions of their lives. Marika describes this need for professional productivity as a demon:

> This thing inside of me is like some alien that I keep feeding. This need to be productive, to produce, weighs me down. Perhaps it is a psychological tumor that needs to be exorcised? I know I am blessed with good fortune in my life, but I can't seem to lift myself off the ground to gain perspective and enjoy the benefits.

Similarly, for Rachel the need to demonstrate her productivity plays out as a form of intellectual paralysis and diminished creativity that pervades her life:

> That pressure, I think affected me is in a very negative way, so I'm not producing more, I'm producing less. I do less work; I don't even read the things anymore I would like to read, so I have this big procrastination problem now because I'm not able to do the work that I really want to spend my time doing, that is valuable to me but that's not valued by our faculty right now, or even by the university, I think, and so then I don't do it at all.

The pressure to perform draws Rachel into areas of research that are productive in terms of scholarship and grants, but not meaningful or intellectually engaging. Her procrastination comes from her lack of desire to take up more traditional forms of scholarship, and results in high levels of anxiety, depression, feelings of incompetence, and compromise to her intellectual integrity.

In contrast, Danielle thrives in compliance with notions of productivity, as she explains, "It's really important for me to overshoot every mark. So if the average is six I want to do ten. If someone is… I don't know, if someone is publishing two articles a year I think, oh well I can do better than that person, I'll publish four." Anna, a sessional instructor with young children, complies with notions of productivity by working at all hours of the day to remain current to compete for a tenure-track job should one become available. She explains how she manages to get her writing done:

> Writing at five in the morning 'til seven in the morning 'til before my children get up, and writing from nine pm to twelve pm – these are not conducive hours to be thinking and publishing. Writing when, despite the fact that you have no money coming in and it's costing me thousands of dollars [e.g., childcare, unpaid work, conference travel, etc.]. I know I'm losing money in order to write, but I do it to make sure that I don't have a gap in my resume…. It's sacrifice in my personal life in terms of spending every waking moment when I'm not with my children as a fulltime mother with very little childcare writing in between these times.

These women are motivated by the demands and pace of academic life and make this their priority. In doing so they perpetuate the normative script of what it means to be a successful academic; however, it is a choice they make and derive satisfaction from their work.

Compromise, Passion, and Desire

> One gaping hole remains in my life – a partner, a companion, someone to love me. I am still seeking validation elsewhere… I have many people who love me and are there for me, yet it isn't enough. I am waiting for prince charming to rescue me and take me away to hide in his castle. I am just so tired of trying to do it all. (Marika)

The women in our study desire love, passion, intimacy, and partnership, but they struggle to let go of the demands of their profession and disposition as an academic to create space to be emotionally available for relationships and intimacy. They are caught in a paradox – the traits that help them to be successful at work tend to undermine their ability to sustain relationships and effectively fulfill other role requirements in their private lives. This is the area of greatest tension in the stories – the compromise in their personal life. Marika describes her struggle in her home life:

> Sometimes I worry because in my work I need to be focused so I make myself emotionally unavailable. I am rational, analytic and hard. There is no space for softness or being vulnerable. When I come home I am expected to shift gears and instantly be that loving, warm and open mother. My husband complains that I am so shut down and hard to reach. It's true; it takes time for me to make the transition.

Similarly, Patti realizes how her work affects her ability to be fully present at home:

> My daughter said, "I don't understand why you're so smart at work and you're so dumb when you come home." I actually think what happens is that because you are so on at work, when you come home you want to relax and not make any decisions…. She saw something I didn't see – that I need to stop and just be.

In a recent *Globe and Mail* newspaper article, a graduate student talks about her divided focus:

> My other home had begun to show signs of neglect. I signed up my son for a gym-
> nastics class and simply forgot to take him to four of the eight classes. Finding it
> much easier to answer the call of an assignment (which had a due date after all) than
> the cry of a tired child who needed a bath and a story. I disappeared to the basement
> night after night; leaving that pleasantly familiar man I lived with to pick up the slack.
> (Kraemer, 2011)

Danielle describes a similar tension of trying to make time for family and work, and she has surrendered her role as primary caregiver to her partner:

> The only way we could make our family and marriage work, because we were both making
> tons of money but were desperately unhappy because neither of us spent much time with
> our children, was for one of us to quit. Someone else was taking care of our children. We'd
> get home and one of us would get supper together while the other would get the kid thing
> done. We weren't happy with that arrangement. After many long conversations with my
> husband, he agreed to give up his career and stay home with the children. We feel that our
> family is meaningful work.

Patti, whose husband left her because the demands of her work were encroaching on their personal lives and marriage, reveals her disappointment: "My biggest regret is I couldn't have both a personal life and my administrative academic life. That's sad."

Some academics have found satisfaction in long-term distant relationships or a lover – both situations provide a specific space and time to be open, vulnerable, and free of commitments of family life and work. Others have channeled their passion into their work and find an element of satisfaction in doing so, and there are some for whom marriage was impossible to negotiate.

Keeping Up Appearances: Wife and Mother

> There are times I want to join the ranks of women who lunch. I want to give it all up and
> become a full-time mother. I am so tired of trying to juggle child-care with contract work,
> publishing and trying to have a life. (Anna)

For those women who are married with children, they find themselves in a con-
tinuous struggle to negotiate their identity and commitment to being an academic
and reconcile the demands and expectations of being a mother and wife. There
is an element of defensiveness, resentment, and sometimes resignation in their
struggle to feel competent in both spheres and demonstrate to themselves and
others that it is possible to do it all. For Anna, who gave up her career to follow
her husband as he advanced in his, there is an underlying tension and resentment.

She explains, "in one breath he'll say 'the next move will be for you' but that never happens, and will never happen, it's very clear" because he reminds her that "when you make the money I make then we'll choose your career." She concludes that given her life situation she will have to come to terms with the situation or leave. She recognizes that she is not yet willing to give up what she has worked so hard to achieve – being a professor and her sense of identity through academia, so she continues to find ways to keep producing.

We are familiar with the narrative of strong academic women challenging the traditional role of wife. Danielle explains:

> One of the reasons I can be successful is because I've got a husband who has been willing to put his career and work on hold for mine. So he's just recently gone back to work. He's completely under employed as a bus driver for a school. So my husband drives a bus. My kids ride the bus with my husband. So we've still found a way to make it work so that our kids are with us, with one of us, but that's a huge cost.

In Danielle's story, there is an acknowledgment of the riskiness of making these choices in terms of her husband's identity and sense of self-worth, and the responsibility that comes with taking on the role as primary income earner. Marika expresses a similar frustration:

> My mother called today to chastise me for being difficult. "You just need to stay home, to go home!" "What do you mean?" I asked. "You need to forget about exercising and being with friends. You need be with your family and get your work done!" My response is two fold. One, I wish I was a housewife and could focus on just being a homemaker, but my husband now does that, so he is viewed as weak and I am a ball buster. Second, I realize that my desire to follow this path to individuality threatens women entrenched in these more traditional roles. So in liberating ourselves we actually work against the oppression created by our mothers and sisters. We threaten their identity and world.

Only recently do we hear counter-narratives that support men who elect to take up the role of primary caregiver and find fulfillment in being a homemaker. High-achieving women in such relationships are viewed as selfish, hard, and driven – abandoning their duties as mother and wife, and rendering their husbands underachievers in the eyes of others.

Alpha Mother: Defending Our Duality

While academic women who choose to also be mothers find satisfaction and joy from this role, it is not without tensions, resistance, and compromise that require them to mindfully manage their time to create the space to take up this responsibility while remaining productive in their professional work. It is with other women where these women experience the need to defend their choice to be a working mother. Anna experiences little support or empathy from her colleagues in her decision to have children:

> You know education is a bizarre faculty, because here we are in the business of teaching teachers about pedagogy and children and yet there's this hostility to being a mother. I sense this hostility of being a mother in an education faculty.... And I can remember, the Dean was female and the hostility every time I got pregnant.

Interestingly, Danielle finds herself being defensive and hostile around mothers who choose to be homemakers:

> I do NOT [emphasis hers] fit in on the playground. Trust me! I can only volunteer in my kids' schools once a month.... If you want me to make cupcakes I will, and I do those kinds of things. You know you're in a different kind of headspace than the way they [full time home-makers/mothers] think. Like in the months that I stayed home [pregnant with second child] they would say things – and I know this is a way to prop up their own self-esteem, but they say things like "oh my goodness, you work so hard, you must find it so hard, you know, to do things at home" or "I haven't seen you at the school lately"; "You know so and so is in piano, and what are you doing with your children?" And I'm like, "Fuck you, get a job. You need a job, you've got too much time on your hands you know."

These stories reflect the common paradox for women who struggle with the multiple demands of femininity – the women reveal the lack of support and encouragement for their role as a mother in their work at the university, while at the same time feeling hostile and angry toward women who choose not to take up this dual struggle.

Fragmented Life

In motherhood, the women in this study seem willing to do whatever it takes to ensure their children's needs are nurtured. For Anna, this means cutting everything but work and children out of her life – "there is no time or energy left for anything else!" Despite this ruthless management of her time, she acknowledges she is frazzled and worn out by the end of the day. She is driving herself crazy to ensure that she can pursue academics while maintaining the pace of a full-time mother:

> There are days where I lose it. I don't know where I'm going, I don't know who I'm picking up – like that happens with anything but I feel it's so exacerbated given that I feel like I'm the primary caregiver because my husband, the nature of his work he's never around. I'm on part time contract, so I don't have a fulltime nanny. I don't have a cleaner because I don't have the money because I'm a sessional, right? So you're kind of doing these things in terms of trying to do it all. That's why I'm saying it's unsustainable, I can't keep this pace up for much longer or else I will crack... pretending that I can have everything together so I'm racing around doing superficial cleans to hide everything and at 11:00 at night I'm starting to make cupcakes for the kindergarten class the next day and you're up until 2:00 in the

morning. And my daughter says, "oh can you make a cake like everybody else does?" And so you're like "sure," and do it.

The internal drive to demonstrate excessive competence in all areas of their lives was a common theme among the participants. Patti remembers how this took a toll on her when she was trying to manage a busy professional life with a young family:

I was just tired… well I know for a fact there was a lot of consideration for my husband. He would say, "I've been busy, I need time, and so you guys just leave me alone." So as a woman… I guess I didn't feel I could ask for that. So I tried to be competent at home. And when in fact I would have been much better off, and [my daughter] said I did it anyway, I was just incompetent at home for awhile and maybe just wouldn't make very many decisions for a day or for half a day.

Danielle has also paid a price for maintaining her desired level of productivity at work at the cost of spending less leisure time with her family. She candidly shares:

I regret it now and you know my kids remind me that we don't spend as much time together as we'd like, as they would like. You know like I'll come home and I get three or four hours a night with my kids. So while my colleagues are writing papers at night or grant applications or whatever, I am happily spending my time with my family you know? So I get up early, at 5:00 or 5:30 every day and try to get an hour of work done before my kids wake up, right? So some of the costs are to me personally, but they're also to my family unit, you know? I really do think you have to work hard as a female faculty member.

These women feel compelled to try to do it all in their role as mother without compromise to their academic careers through aggressively compartmentalizing their life into manageable roles, tasks, and events. Both Marika and Danielle planned marriage and childbirth around their career. Marika got married and pregnant during the final year of her doctoral degree and began teaching when her daughter was two months old. Danielle reasoned that because of the enormous pressure involved in the tenure process she delayed marriage: "We got married because we wanted to have children, and I wouldn't get married until I had tenure. I said 'too bad, you've got to wait'… so I got tenure, had an ulcer, and found out I was pregnant all in the same month." She reveals her frustration at not being able to control this as efficiently as she would have liked:

It took us a year and a half [to get pregnant], right after making the decision. And I think it's partly because of this place. It's so god damn busy that you really do disrupt your feminine cycles. I have no scientific proof of that, it's just that okay and I mean maybe it's just the way it is with a lot of women that are working full time, I don't know, but it took us like a year and a half.

Anna recounts, "I can remember planning when I would conceive my child so it would end the week after [academic term]… so that I could come back to work before fall term started." None of these women entertained the possibility of taking their full maternity leave; instead, they plan their private life around the academic year to meet the expectations of the academy.

Hard Choices

These women are motivated by fear of being perceived as not able to manage the pace and demands of academic work, a fear that has not been realized by any of them, yet they ruthlessly self-monitor to ensure they never falter in their work productivity. They continue to play within the rules they understand, even if this means sacrifice in other areas of their lives. Marika reflects on how this rigidity has resulted in a deep fear to follow her passion and work in areas that may not be in the mainstream:

> I think my greatest weakness is a lack of courage to take risks, to push myself to move beyond the limits of safety, and to unleash my potential: To fly alone. I am 44 years old and I will give myself 6 years to find my wings and really fly. When I am 50 I want to be viewed as having done important work. The truth is I am used to success, so to be vulnerable takes courage.

Like many successful academic women, the women in this study present to the professional world their competence and resilience. This extreme competence comes at a cost, often a deep sense of tiredness that sometimes extends into depression. Marika shares, "I fight the slip back into depression. What is it about being back at the university that takes me there? I am experiencing an eclipse of confidence in my whole life – in how I look, in my work and in my place in this world. I have not yet found my way and I don't know why." There is a disjuncture between the personal/private sphere and the professional sphere in the lives of many academic women. For these women, choosing to live a fragmented life inevitably leads to tiredness, burnout, sometimes depression, and tension in their primary relationships.

LIMINAL SPACES

What does it mean to be academic women with full and rich lives of work, family, and fulfilling personal relationships? Reading the story of these women's struggle and resistance reveals the constraints that structure their sense of self and limit opportunities to live their lives in ways they desire. We ponder the transformative potential inherent in the periods of liminality described by these women, where they are betwixt and between roles and responsibilities, as an opportunity to express individuality, consider other pathways, and what might constitute a more integrated life. Rachel, Marika, and Patti experience deep dissatisfaction with what might be viewed as an inauthentic life – driven by external demands, rather than their own desires. They question their competence and secure identity in both their professional and personal life. They have come to a point in their lives where they experience the lack of a secure identity that is expressed in their feelings of being lost, free falling, of not belonging, causing anxiety, fear, and depression. This liminal space, however, can also be a space of transformation, a resting space to clarify self-concept, resolve inner conflict, and reflect on desire. Heilbrun (1999) reminds us that it is at the threshold, often an unknown and dangerous space characterized by instability, where women can write the new narratives for their lives. The stories we have heard are not uncommon to high-achieving women. It is in the process of writing and sharing these private struggles that we find support and community to consider our lives might be otherwise. We gain practical wisdom from these stories of fellow travelers regarding how to overcome the challenges in choosing particular pathways. We have a richer understanding of the private and professional consequences of choosing to follow the dominant scripts for academics, and may contemplate a pathway to pursue research that may not be as lucrative in terms of grants and output – to seek more life-work balance, and to find satisfaction in a journey toward an undivided life (Palmer, 2004).

We argue that as academic women challenged with the double entanglement of intellectual work and the demands of femininity, we need to share our stories publicly, as a way of removing the veil of secrecy between our private and professional spheres. Through this unveiling, we can begin to challenge our stories and explore the ways in which we are either limited or set free by the narratives that shape our lives. We can then cultivate counter-narratives that provide insight into our interior and private lives to inform our collective memories of the full account of the lives of high-achieving, successful academic women. Heilbrun (1988) explains:

> What matters is that lives do not serve as models; only stories do that. And it is a hard thing to make up stories to live by. We can only retell and live by the stories we have read or heard. We live our lives through texts. They may be read, or chanted, or experienced electronically, or come to us, like the murmurings of our mothers, telling us what conventions demand. Whatever their form or medium, these stories have formed us all; they are what we must use to make new fictions, new narratives. (p. 37)

CONCLUSION

> I am so very fragile. Like a little bird that has been caged for a long time and one day realizes the cage door is open. She hops out onto a branch. It is a crispy frozen winter day. The air is silent, the sky is blue and everything is frozen still. The little bird rests on the branch of a

tree, hardened by the frozen rain of yesterday. Her heart is beating in her chest. She rests to take in the possibilities of freedom. Then suddenly the branch snaps with a combination of her weight and the warming of the sun. Snap, snap, the ice crystals fall from the trees and it is as if the beautiful world begins to crumble around her. She is free falling, forgetting that she has wings, that she can rescue herself. (Marika)

As women academics we have been socialized to be achievement focused, self-disciplined, and driven to do it all. We make sacrifices in our personal lives, delaying marriage and having children, in our pursuit of tenure and promotion. We know that we have limited time to prove ourselves, to acquire the accomplishments necessary to qualify for tenure and promotion, so we carefully manage our private lives to coincide with the needs of the work. We are unwilling to compromise our role as mothers, so we strive to schedule our lives around the need to be productive – up at 5:00 a.m. to write until the kids are awake and back to work once they are in bed.

We are aware that the demands of academic life require compromise, particularly for women who struggle to balance them with the responsibilities and expectations of femininity – being a mother, partner, and daughter. However, in keeping our stories hidden we lose the opportunity to shape new stories that could reframe our struggles for a more positive transformational potential. The realities of balancing the multiple demands may not necessarily shift, but we can begin to frame our lives from a sense of agency and purpose through our individual and collective narratives. We can make choices to perpetuate the second or third shift, we can try to find more balance by sharing domestic work with our partners, or we can speak up to bring about change, to redefine what it means to be productive and create measures or benchmarks indicating what is enough. In this way, our stories could become a source for inspiration, support, and hope (Marso, 2006).

Telling our stories of struggle, resistance, surrender, and the consequences lets us know we are not alone in our attempt do it all. As academics, like the rest of humankind, we seek inclusion, affirmation, and a sense of belonging to a greater community of like-minded souls. Our intent is to co-create spaces for dialogue and story-sharing as we strive to dissemble power differentials and contribute to the sustainability of healthy communities where we can flourish as intellectual women and contributing members.

NOTE

1   This chapter is reprinted from *Women's Studies International Forum*, Vol. 45, Cherkowski, Sabre, and Lynn Bosetti, "Behind the Veil: Academic Women Negotiating Demands of Femininity," pp. 19–26, Copyright (2014), with permission from Elsevier.

CHAPTER SIX

On the Educational Value of Philosophical Ethics

A Reflection on the Problem of "Relevance" in Teacher Education[1]

CHRISTOPHER MARTIN

INTRODUCTION AND OVERVIEW

In keeping with scholarly theme of "contested sites in higher education," the aim of this chapter is to undertake a serious exploration of the extent to which, and ways in which, philosophical ethics can articulate its educational value for teacher candidates in a higher education climate that is preoccupied with the notion of "relevance." How can philosophers of education conceptualize, and account for, their ethical work with teachers?

In this chapter, I present an overview of various approaches to thinking about the value of philosophical ethics and assess the extent to which those approaches express its educational potential. I then advance and defend an account of my own, arguing that the best way to do this is to understand moral inquiry about education as an intellectual tradition into which teachers ought to be initiated.

Context of the Inquiry

Many of the chapters in this volume focus on the personal challenges and struggles faced by academics working in a changing educational landscape. Philosophers of education are not exempt from such changes. Higher education reform has affected the field in at least two important ways.

First, change in the cultural and political climate of higher education has led to an increasing emphasis on the idea that publicly funded research should lead to measurable outcomes. Recent developments in the UK under the Research Excellence Framework (REF), for example, suggest that future funding schemes will grant "significant additional recognition… where researchers build on excellent research to deliver demonstrable benefits to the economy, society, public policy, culture and quality of life" (HECFE, 2009). How exactly are philosophers of education expected to demonstrate such benefits? Who assesses such demonstrations? What about philosophers of education whose work is not so "demonstrably" beneficial or relevant?

Second, the philosophy of education has always had an applied focus emphasizing the implications of various philosophical commitments for such wide-ranging practical issues as curriculum development in moral education, the just distribution of educational resources, and the normative criteria of quality in education. Historically, philosophers working in the field in the 1960s and 1970s were able to directly influence the conceptual schemes of candidate teachers through their active participation in and contribution to teacher education programs (Hirst, 1965; Peters, 1966; White, 1982). Scholarly work and the university setting was, in this sense, a proxy for education policy (Oancea & Bridges, 2009). Today, however, the growing emphasis in educational reform on the standardized assessment of instruction and teacher accountability has left teachers with increasingly less discretion in terms of professional judgment, and so much of the direction of educational policy in many countries such as Canada, the United States, and UK is driven at the state level (Pring, 2007). Consequently, philosophers of education have since focused their attention to more indirect areas of influence such as the philosophy of educational research and curriculum theory (White, 2012; Winch, 2012; for a discussion of the ethical dimensions of "relevance" in the context of philosophical work on educational policy see Martin, 2011).

Policy analysis and critique, then, are understandably a growing area of focus for philosophers of education. The policy arena is seemingly more open to critique and scholarly intervention than teacher education and practice, making it seemingly easier to make a case for "benefit" and "relevance." Despite this meritorious focus on policy, however, I believe that philosophers of education may be too hasty to pursue policy "relevance" at the expense of teacher preparation. Philosophers of education still have much of educational value to offer teacher candidates, even in a climate of serious deprofessionalization. Such value is worth defending. What is needed is a clear and substantive account, not simply of why ethics matters in education, but why *philosophical ethics* is worthwhile on educational grounds.

I will examine some of the major approaches to philosophical ethics in teacher education in an effort to assess its educational value for teacher candidates. While what follows involves a scholarly, educationalist critique of philosophical ethics, my own experiences have greatly marked the line of inquiry undertaken here. All philosophers of education struggle to find a synthesis between the practical concerns of teacher candidates, on the one hand, and the philosophical understanding that is essential for such candidates to engage in those practical concerns in a meaningful, just, and ethical way, on the other. What follows is an attempt at just such a synthesis.

THE MORAL DOMAIN AND TEACHER EDUCATION CURRICULA

What contribution can we expect to make when we talk about philosophical ethics with teachers? The specificity of this question is meant to distinguish it from the more common view that philosophical ethics is necessary for professionals to "know ethics." The growth in research on education as a moral enterprise has emphasised that teaching requires more than mere regulation via professional codes or general principles (Goodlad, Soder, & Sirotnik, 1990; Sanger, 2008; Stengel & Tom, 1995). Accordingly, in this section I will expand on some of the ways a philosophical ethics curriculum can enact the relationship between the moral domain of education and teacher practice.

Philosophical Ethics as a Selective Account of Teacher Practice

One approach could be to use philosophical ethics to derive a particular conception of teacher practice. If philosophers and educational theorists can develop persuasive arguments about what teaching ought to be, it may be possible to promote a shift away from the educational narrowness entailed by a growing accountability and measurement culture (see Huebner, 1996, for an example of this approach). A philosophical ethics of the emotions, for example, might promote in teacher candidates a deeper conceptual understanding and awareness of caring relationships with students in ways that an ethics of accountability, so dominant in professional culture today, might undermine.

However, the unintended consequence of this approach may be the overturning of an uncritical acceptance of a dominant, received notion of good teacher practice, only to have it replaced with another. For example, a teacher education program modeled on a Murdochian ethics, focused on the development of a teacher's "inner life" and moral experience, may not be entirely sufficient when the teacher's ability to publicly explain or justify his or her decisions to parents, students, and the community may also be an important dimension of good teaching practice. On the other hand, a rationalistic conception of ethics that emphasizes the justifiability of ethical action may elide the more complex and intimate ethical terrain of the classroom environment. Drawing on a particular ethical tradition can exclude other moral considerations that may be representative of other educational aims or aspects of good teaching practice.

Philosophical Ethics as a Selective Account of the Moral Life

Another approach is to use philosophical ethics to reinforce a particular understanding of what it means to live an ethical life, and then explore what living an ethical life means for teachers. Here we start with the general and move to the particular. But what understanding of the ethical life is the proper one? When an ethic of justice, an ethic of care, and an ethic of social change are each posited as competing accounts of the moral domain, an overgeneralization about how we ought to act in the classroom context may arise. Some normative conceptions, for example, may privilege teachers as carers while mischaracterizing justice as an uncaring, and undesirable, form of rational detachment. Yet, for teachers who see their task as drawing students into a positive learning experience, elements of care, fairness, nurturance, and reflection may play a role in different ways and at different stages. A teacher can care for each individual student's progress while also being committed to the idea that all students ought to have an equal opportunity to contribute to their own progress.

In other words, philosophical ethics is by its nature going to be selective about those features of the classroom that teachers should attend to, morally. Such selectivity is just what we want teachers in their moral preparation to be able to do. But it is important to ensure that philosophical ethics is not reductive by virtue of this selectivity – that such selectivity does not lead us to ignore those features of moral life that ought not to be ignored (Louden, 1992). When philosophical ethics is taught in a reductionist way it undermines our efforts at teacher preparation and may even undermine appropriate and well-grounded moral intuitions. For example, the good teacher may already recognize that classroom practices need to be grounded in considerations such as justice – that the provision of education to all children is a morally just tradition of which the teacher is taking part – but also recognizes that particular moments in the classroom require more than a sense of justice as learning processes take shape. Such a shaping is itself an ethical matter because the teacher is working with students in directing their learning in presumably worthwhile ways. Focusing on a justice-centered ethics alone may lead to a neglect of these other ethical dimensions.

Philosophical Ethics Between Moral Life and Moral Practice

These tensions seem to suggest that teacher educators find themselves between the horns of dilemma when they seek to use philosophical ethics to promote thought and reflection about the moral dimension of their work. As Weinert's (2001) pragmatic analysis of educational concepts has shown, what we teach in the professional context risks becoming intellectually trivial or pragmatically useless if not anchored in ways that reflect the practices to which they are applied. This entails a difficult balance from the standpoint of curriculum development. Educationally worthwhile concepts must reflect a set of specifiable tasks that anyone who wishes to undertake a specific practice must master, but yet must also stay true to the overarching ethical frame of value within which the practice is situated (see Kole, 2011, for an example of this kind of analysis in professional education). For example, teachers may be tasked with specific institutionalized goals and learning objectives but the reasons for undertaking such objectives must resonate with a broader sense of moral purpose to which the enterprise of education belongs.

What this means is that, from an educational point of view, philosophical ethics must be broad enough to equip teachers with an understanding of the distinctly moral character of education. However, in its broadness these ethical concepts can become so abstract that it becomes unclear just how they are to be applied in the context of practice. For example, educating for a basic conceptual understanding of a principle such as "respect for persons" might capture a great deal of the moral life. It is not altogether clear and easy to know how respect should play out in the classroom context where discipline and classroom management is required, especially for novice teachers. The philosophical and ethical concepts that we expect teachers to engage with must be made to connect to practices in ways that are instructive and meaningful to them.

And yet, focusing too narrowly on the practice can be problematic as well – for example, in keeping the remit of ethical preparation to institutionalized codes of teacher conduct. On this approach, the teacher of philosophical ethics acts as an expert whose job is simply to infer a set of desirable behaviors from ethical theory and convince the teacher of the merits of these behaviors (for an account of such an approach in the context of expertise in educational research, see Floden, 1985). In focusing on the specifics of the practice in this way, philosophical ethics collapses into a list of behaviors that leave the underlying norms and values informing such behaviors underdetermined and unexamined. Ironically, such a pedagogical approach has the potential to divorce teachers' actions from ethical traditions and aims that motivate their work in the first place.

All this suggests a dialectical tension between the perceived abstraction of values articulated by different philosophical traditions, on the one hand, and the specific tasks that we want professionals to be able to competently accomplish, on the other. One common way of addressing this tension in a variety of professions is the "applied ethical theory" approach. Here, we teach professionals to learn how to use moral concepts to arrive at determinate answers to specific situations in which they might find themselves. A paradigmatic example of an applied approach is found in the works of Kenneth Strike and Jonas Soltis (Strike, 1990; Strike & Soltis, 1985). They adopt several moral concepts that are seen in their view to be most commonly required for good professional practice, such as due process, but seek to avoid the requirement that students engage significantly with the philosophical traditions from which those concepts originate (Strike, 1990). A similar approach has been adopted in the context of medical ethics teaching in the well-known "Georgetown Mantra" of biomedical principles. Here, fixed sets of principles are presented in isolation from the philosophical-ethical traditions that originate them (Beauchamp & Childress, 1979). However, this "decontextualized" approach has been extensively critiqued for failing to address either side of the dilemma: Applied approaches are seen as too abstract to offer anything of use to non-philosopher practitioners. Yet they are also thought by some to be too narrow in offering specific, reductive, and often rigorist conceptions of the moral life and moral value (Caplan, 1983; Howe, 1986; Kymlicka, 1993; Putnam, 1983; Watras, 1986).

Regardless of the validity or cogency of these critiques, the applied ethical approach is insufficient for our specific context of concern – the case for the educational value of educational concepts for teachers. Decontextualizing ethical concepts from philosophical-ethical traditions discounts the potential disciplinary contribution of those traditions to understanding the moral domain – on the applied approach philosophical ethics is simply the wellspring from which practically useful concepts flow. Yet, the disciplinary contribution of moral philosophy and theory may be essential for teachers, especially if they are to develop a moral perspective on their practice that is not simply grounded in intuition or subjective preference (Campbell, 1997), or only in the authority of the curricula as it is presented to them. Furthermore, if teachers see ethical inquiry as a mere matter of applying a finite set of concepts to cases, the possibility for such inquiry to make a meaningful contribution to teacher understanding is significantly limited. Teachers may come to believe that ethical reflection is exhausted through the application of concepts such as due process or fairness as required. Yet, the task of teaching and the development of the student already presuppose a set of moral commitments that involve continual (re)enactment of ethical understanding. Our concern is with the educational contribution of philosophical ethics to an understanding of the moral dimensions of teaching – the ways in which teachers come to see themselves and their work as a matter of distinct moral agency. Such a contribution is valuable insofar as it is meaningful and identifies something important about the ever-present moral life to be found in teacher practice, something not entirely expressed in learning a limited complement of ethical concepts that apply to commonly encountered cases (as practically useful as such concepts at times may be).

THE MORAL IS IN THE PRACTICE

Given these various complications, perhaps the dialectic can be resolved by bypassing philosophical ethics altogether. This is the direction taken by philosophers such as David Hansen. Hansen (1998) claims that societal disagreement about "values" makes teachers uncomfortable with seeing their work as moral and philosophical disagreements only compound the problem (p. 644). Hansen thinks that much of the problem lies in the attempt to secure the moral value of teaching by importing aims and values that are "external" to teaching practice (p. 646). On his view, philosophical accounts of teaching erroneously "plug in" whatever we want from education and derive moral worth from teaching practice on this basis.

For Hansen (1998), the source of this problematic conception of moral value lies in the premise that teachers can choose between different accounts of moral value, where what counts as moral in teaching is based on contingent and subjective beliefs that may orient teaching practice in different ways depending on what those beliefs are. On Hansen's account, these interchangeable, "external" beliefs about moral value miss the mark. Rather, the moral source of teaching is generated from the tradition of the practice itself: "[T]eacher educators can derive the moral dimensions of teaching from pondering the practice itself, rather than from having to turn first to particular moral theories or political ideologies, to particular societal or cultural values, or to any other source external to and conceived apart from the work of teachers" (p. 647).

Hansen's (1998) proposal suggests a promising pedagogy. If we can uncover the moral in teaching practice, teacher educators and candidates will acquire an awareness of the moral dimensions of classroom phenomena insofar as they understand what teaching really is as a practice. On this view, an understanding of the moral value of teaching develops through a process of discovery as one is initiated into the practice itself: "[T]eachers quickly discover, if they are serious-minded, that moral qualities such as patience, attentiveness, and fairness are built into teaching" (p. 649). On this quasi-Aristotelian view, the moral dimensions of teaching are discovered as the teacher candidate acquires the right motives, learns to use the necessary means, and adopts the appropriate dispositions required to successfully pursue his or her craft.

Hansen's (1998) description of teacher practice infused with intrinsic moral value is an attractive one and certainly seems to accord with the sensibilities of "serious-minded" teachers. Without the requisite motives (such as acting out of the best interests of students) and dispositions (patience, attentiveness, fair-mindedness) teachers will be hard-pressed to be successful in the pursuit of their craft. However, if we grant Hansen's claim that the practice of teaching is necessarily home to the values, aims, and relationships that make the moral worth of teaching possible to begin with, it does not necessarily follow that these values, aims, and relationships are themselves justifiable from a moral perspective, nor does it entail that that these values, aims, and relationships are self-justifying, or *prima facie* valid over other values, aims, and relationships. While broad aims such as "growth" and "broadening horizons" may be necessary for orienting teacher practice, it is by no means epistemically clear as to why and when these aims take precedence over other aims or values.

Hansen (1998) attempts to anticipate just such an objection:

> [One] might say that my argument is tautological... that I have simply described a set of moral features of teaching and that, surprise!, we need go no further than to teaching itself to identify and articulate those moral features.... My main response to this criticism is that theory is not the only way to derive the moral. (p. 650)

Hansen attributes this criticism to a "long-standing assumption" that we first need philosophy to tell us what is moral (p. 650). If this is indeed the role that moral theory has handed itself, we might best steer clear from philosophical ethics.

Nonetheless, there are at least two good reasons for not settling on the notion that practices themselves originate, determine, or supply their own standards of moral or ethical value, and these are good reasons regardless of our conception of the purpose of moral philosophy. The first has to do with the sources of normativity in Hansen's conception of teacher practice. Theoretically, his account does not explain where these moral values came from in the first place. On what grounds, for example, did teachers originally distinguish permissible and impermissible, or good and bad, aspects of their craft as the tradition evolved? The practice-based approach is not clear on how such decisions could come about from appeal to the internal workings of the practice alone, especially when we consider that in this case the internal workings of the practice were only in the process of being worked out by teachers.

Even if one could develop an explanatory model for how such values arise from the structure of teacher practice, it does not seem possible to justify Hansen's (1998) conception without appeal to moral values that have a life prior to, independent of, and beyond the practice of teaching itself. Hansen claims the moral value of teaching is something that cannot be chosen – schools can choose to ignore these moral values, "but to do so means abandoning the practice in favour of something else" (p. 651). However, if the moral is only in the practice, how can Hansen justify his belief that teacher practice in the form developed by him is of greater worth versus competing conceptions of classroom practice (think, for example, of outcome-based conceptions of classroom practice dominant today)? It seems that he must either show that his conception of teaching is more effective in "getting results" (an instrumental justification that obviates the argument for moral value to begin with) or make an appeal to more general values that extend beyond the practice.

Second, I have already pointed out that normative descriptions of teacher practice are contested entities. Beginning with a particular description of teacher practice as authoritative has the potential to reinforce already-present ideological tendencies or close teaching off from critical perspectives or further moral insight. Hansen (1998) is right to suggest that moral philosophy is unhelpful when it arbitrarily "articulates the desired ends first" and then imports that meaning into teaching. However, this same kind of unhelpfulness can also be attributed to approaches that articulate the desired practices first and then import the moral aims of teaching from those same descriptions.

Nonetheless, there is something crucial in Hansen's (1998) emphasis on the practice as serving home to moral self-understanding. I take him to be recognizing that understanding teaching (and education generally) as a distinctly moral endeavor requires *content* – an account of just what it is that teachers do that would make it worth being labeled "moral" to begin with. Such a description is itself a *moral* description and is already infused with moral language. Professional ethics as a set of moral insights that are applied to amoral practices, as if from a distance, is ineffectual or even counterproductive in ways that parallel the Hegelian critique of formalism in moral theory. Hegel's objection was that by focusing exclusively on abstract rules, concepts, principles, and codes we become increasingly unable to come to terms with morality as a practice that is always situated in real contexts of interaction with others (for an example of the Hegelian tradition as applied to teacher ethics see Stojanov, 2009). So too, I think, is there the danger entailed by a similarly disconnected pedagogy of professional ethics where teachers are disinclined to understand teaching as a kind of always-present morality-in-practice.

PHILOSOPHICAL ETHICS AS MORAL PLURALISM

A third alternative is to return to philosophical ethics, but in a more organic way – one that avoids the purported abstraction and formalism of applied ethics. Strike (1999) suggests this approach within the context of debates on the relative priority of justice and care in the classroom:

> [J]ustice and caring aim at different moral goods, they may conflict. When teachers grade, they may wish to encourage, and they may wish to give each student what he or she deserves. They may not be able to do both. One account of such a conflict is moral pluralism. Moral pluralism says that moral goods are irreducibly many and often conflict. It is part of the human condition and we cannot achieve every good fully in every situation. (p. 21)

On this view, the classroom is a morally complex environment and any account of the moral dimensions of teaching must be inclusive in terms of the "moral goods" identified. If relationships are essential to teaching practice, the fostering and preservation of healthy relationships may have relevance in our moral deliberations. Similarly, there will be times when equality of treatment will have greater relevance. By acquainting teachers with different normative theories without subordinating one to the other, they can become aware of the various facets of the moral nature of their work as a diverse picture of the classroom begins to form. If we adopt a moral pluralist approach to philosophical ethics, it follows that we can promote a more comprehensive awareness of the moral dimensions of teaching. By "comprehensive" I mean that the more normative perspectives on the classroom environment we learn about, the more diverse and inclusive our moral considerations will be. The broader our conceptual net, the larger our moral catch.

This account seems to accord with our pedagogical intuitions about teaching ethics. For example, many ethics teachers use case studies to arrive at a broad conceptual distinction between consequentialism and non-consequentialism. Once students can distinguish between the consequences of an action versus acting from obligation in accordance to principle, a new dimension of classroom life begins to emerge. This is valuable because teacher candidates may be generally well aware that the consequences of an action are morally significant (e.g., pain, punishment, hurt feelings). However, they may be less aware that acting on principle where consequences are not decisive is also a morally significant consideration. The aim here is not to direct students toward viewing in the abstract either consequences or principles as having greater moral worth. Rather, in true moral pluralist fashion, the aim is to encourage them to recognize, at a conceptual level, that there are morally significant phenomena other than consequences. Accordingly, a broad conception of philosophical ethics can promote an awareness of a variety of morally relevant conceptual distinctions.

However, while moral pluralism may encourage greater moral-conceptual awareness of a particular environment such as the classroom, it may be of no help when moral values conflict. In fact, a comprehensive account of moral value, paradoxically, places *greater* demands on our ability to make reflective ethical judgments – moral pluralism, after all, reveals many diverse and conflicting goods.

A distinction between moral salience and moral judgment brings this out. A perception of moral salience is essentially an expression of our moral upbringing – the accretion of the moral values, rules, and principles we have come to internalize through our ongoing socialization. Consider, for example, the many case studies we use when teaching ethics. Case studies are instructional because they flag a need for moral judgment. It is a sense of moral salience that allows us to recognize that the situation requires judgment in the first place (Herman, 1996). Asking whether it is morally right or not to compel an anxious child to participate in a school play presupposes that we have learned at some point to recognize that stress is potentially harmful (especially so) for children. While teacher candidates are able to recognize a certain degree of moral salience by virtue of their socialization they need to be encouraged to be more sensitive to such features in contexts, such as the classroom, where they are dealing with vulnerable children.

However, moral salience itself has no final moral or justificatory authority. The values, rules, and principles we have been socialized into can be mistaken or harmful to others and at the least require justification. This is what I think moral pluralists such as Strike (1999) are suggesting when they argue that we need to find a "reasoned balance" when different moral conceptions compete (p. 36). But what would such a reasoned balance consist in? If the values, rules, and principles we have been socialized into are possibly mistaken or harmful, how is balancing between them going to be reasonable, or serve as a corrective? It has been noted that such an approach is not altogether clear under what conditions one moral good would "inappropriately" rule over another on moral pluralist grounds (Martin, 2011). When philosophical ethics are conceived along pluralist lines, insufficient pedagogical guidance is offered for critical reflection or deliberation on the appropriate grounds for assessing these different conceptions. We thus risk leaving students with the perception that such values are a matter of individual preference or that balance is a fundamentally pragmatic consideration for the teacher.

LIBERAL EDUCATION AND CONFLICTING GOODS

A tension between moral theory and teacher practice has produced a series of educational challenges with respect to the application of philosophical ethics to teacher preparation (enhanced understanding of specific cases, focusing on the practice, seeking a balance among goods). The educational debates animated by this tension have largely focused on articulating aims or outcomes that would justify the teaching of philosophical ethics – the need to promote moral salience of the classroom environment, a fostering of specific understandings of teacher practice, an improved ability to deal with common but challenging cases. To be sure, a program of professional education should have a clear list of objectives that any educator who undertakes such a program should achieve. However, contributing in such a direct fashion is not an appropriate way of applying, in educationally worthwhile ways, moral theory and philosophical ethics – as we have seen, such theories are not really designed to bring about such aims and outcomes. They do not, as Hansen (1998) rightly suggests, serve to tell us what is moral as if we were blank slates before encountering moral theory. Philosophical ethics, as a body of inquiry, represents an ongoing attempt to clarify the various features of our moral understanding, psychology, and experience. This includes being able to apply a moral perspective – which can include one's moral intuitions and commitments – in reasonable and critically reflective ways. I therefore defend that view that the educational value of philosophical ethics is best brought to fruition by applying it in ways that are consistent with what a moral theory or philosophical ethic is trying to achieve or represent – an ongoing learning process of moral thought, inquiry, and practice. This learning process is best promoted within the framework of liberal education.

The ideal of a liberal education in philosophical ethics originates in part in the complexity of choosing among moral goods in an increasingly diverse, complex, and pluralistic society. This is just the political, ethical, and practical challenge that liberal philosophers of education identified in their own body of work. Liberal philosophy of education gained significant prominence in moral, political, and educational philosophy throughout the twentieth century. Philosophers such as Michael Oakshott, R. S. Peters, and Paul Hirst all cogently argued for the crucial role that an initiation into the values, forms of knowledge, and processes of inquiry definitive of the sciences, arts, and humanities can play in addressing the complexity of modern life.

Of particular relevance here is R. S. Peters. Peters rightly pointed out that in a diverse society it becomes increasingly difficult to undertake a clear assessment of why someone ought to learn X versus learning Y. Having been acquainted with many different values and worthwhile activities, how can we equip persons to make reasoned choices among such values? Peters argues that the answer lies in the asking of the question. In asking which particular values one should choose, one presupposes that one must acquire the more general understandings required for making such an assessment. These general understandings just are those values required for making assessments of value. For liberal philosophers of education these basic values are best embodied through traditions of knowledge and understanding such as science, art, and philosophy (Peters, 1966; Giffiths & Peters, 1962). On this view, these traditions of understanding serve as an overarching educational framework necessary for making particular judgments and this defines the pedagogy of a liberal education – we ought to be initiated into forms of understanding, themselves part of an holistic, extended, and ongoing learning process necessary for making value judgments in an increasingly complex modernity.

Such an argumentation strategy is not a matter of question-begging or infinite regress. What Peters is trying to suggest is that reflecting critically about what is good or worthwhile cannot be achieved by learning about a set of particular goods or worthwhile activities. In the course of such learning a student must be initiated into the basic contours of what it means to consider or assess something to be good or worthwhile – through what Peters called "principles of procedure" that are at the core of any liberal education such as respect for persons, toleration, and deciding matters through discussion as opposed to force (Peters, 1973, p. 126). Peters believed that science, literature, and philosophy are learning traditions that are ideally suited to fostering an appreciation of such principles in students and therefore warranted their inclusion in the liberal curricula.

Peters's views on the content of a liberal education have undergone significant scrutiny over the years, particularly in his belief that theoretical knowledge such as science is key to understanding principles of procedure (Hand, 2009; White, 1973; Wilson, 1979). However, Peters's broader views on liberal education continue to play an influential role and I propose that a similar argumentation strategy can be applied in ways that can disclose the educational value of philosophical ethics for teachers.

PHILOSOPHICAL ETHICS AS LIBERAL EDUCATION

Clearly, teachers need to be acquainted with a variety of conceptions of moral value. However, there will be cases in which these moral goods or values conflict. Applying the liberal education argument to philosophical ethics suggests that in asking which moral goods one must choose, one must acquire the moral understandings required for making such an assessment. But such understandings do not consist in familiarity with a list of "good acts," a finite set of moral concepts or descriptions of good teacher practices. Rather, teachers need to engage in principles of procedure that that are definitive of any assessment of moral value. In other words, philosophical ethics serves as a means to moral understanding as a learning tradition of inquiry and reflection, a tradition that needs to be applied to the classroom environment if we are to more fully appreciate this context as a site for ongoing moral learning and engagement.

What exactly would the principles of procedure that are supposed to serve as the framework for such an approach consist in or look like? Developments in modern moral philosophy have begun to articulate the principles underlying such an approach in some detail. Recent work has sought to respond to moral pluralism, for example, by emphasizing procedural principles of reflection and deliberation, not simply as desirable character traits but as a necessary requirement for moral understanding. Such work contends that deliberative procedures entail an important set of conceptual, cognitive, and affective competencies for any moral agent (Rehg, 2003). For example, work in this area has focused on the public nature of moral reasoning where deliberative principles of reciprocity, symmetry, and inclusion must be met (Bohman, 1996; Habermas, 1990; Haydon, 1986). These principles require moral agents to be responsive to the reasons other give when deliberating on an ethical question. Such conditions or principles are seen to align closely to what Peters had in mind by "principles of procedure" as applied to the educational domain and demonstrate the extent to which the moral life must itself be a learning process (Martin, 2009). The ethical preparation of teachers requires that they be able to apply this learning process to their own teacher practice once understood as a distinct moral entity. It should therefore be of little surprise that it is increasingly acknowledged that teacher candidates require more opportunities to experience principled deliberation and reflection about their practice in ways that can develop a reflective and *educative* moral attitude about that practice (de Ruyter & Kole, 2010). For recent developments in this kind of work, see Graham Haydon's account of public morality, or "morality in the narrow sense," and the educational implications of such a conception (Haydon, 1999, 2011).

How exactly do we acquaint teachers with a tradition of moral understanding and inquiry defined by principles of procedure? We can see philosophical ethics here as playing an analogous role to the forms of understanding in Peters's account of liberal education. Here, ethical reflection and deliberation focused on the application of various normative frameworks in addressing the moral dimensions of teaching promote initiation into those principles of procedure, such as reciprocity and symmetry, that are necessary for understanding what it is to make moral judgments in the first place. Yet, initiation into such a tradition of inquiry invites us to systematically assess the various implications of different ethical accounts in the classroom context and can show teacher candidates how we should think about the moral life of the classroom specifically. This systematic assessment goes beyond moral pluralism because the liberal approach is predicated on ethical inquiry as an ongoing learning process toward moral understanding whereas moral pluralism is predicated on the view that ethical inquiry is simply a means to adjudicating between conflicting goods.

To be sure, a liberal education of philosophical ethics serves as a framework for or supplement to, but not replacement of, the many other aspects of professional ethics education. But how should specific ethical traditions, such as those inspired by Levinas or Kant, Mill, Murdoch, or Aristotle, contribute to such an education? On a liberal education view we ought to seek these perspectives as contributions, effected through principles of procedure such as argumentation and perspective-taking, to a broader conversation aimed at a better understanding of moral life. Initiation into this broader tradition through a variety of ethical frameworks is fundamental to understanding moral judgment because this tradition has come to embody basic values that are essential for learning about moral life to begin with – values such as reciprocity, reasoned reflection, and affective concern for others. Applying such efforts to teaching will not end philosophical disagreement over the moral domain of education but it does offer a framework with which teachers can begin to comprehensively address a variety of moral issues without supposing that such comprehensiveness entails a subjective or pragmatic attitude.

LIBERAL EDUCATION AND TEACHER PRACTICE: BRINGING TEACHING AND MORALITY INTO CONTACT

The liberal education approach interprets the tensions between philosophical ethics and teacher practice as two learning processes that overlap and mutually reinforce one another. This is where Hansen's (1998) emphasis on teaching practice dovetails with an appropriately conceived pedagogy of philosophical ethics. The tradition of teaching and the tradition of moral reflection need to be put back into contact with each other. The decline of comprehensive education in the broader postsecondary context, combined with the emphasis on the mastery of specific techniques and policies within teacher education, suggest that such generative contact is needed more than ever before. A liberal education approach can facilitate such generative contact in two important ways.

First, defenders of the procedural interpretation of moral deliberation recognize that principles of procedure cannot generate their own content, nor can they offer a description of what our practices ought to be. The development of any conception of teaching as a distinctly moral endeavor therefore requires engagement with the existing motivations, intuitions, beliefs, and practices. A liberal pedagogy of philosophical ethics does not aim to transcend teacher practice but works to ensure that traditions of moral inquiry work with traditions of teacher practice over and against initiatives that do not accord with any reasonable understanding of a teacher's moral obligations. The practice of teaching is an ethical tradition to which "external" or ideologically driven aims and objectives should not be arbitrarily introduced, context-free. On a liberal view, reforms that seek to overhaul teaching under the banner of management and accountability need to make good *moral* arguments for their validity. Such arguments must be made through engagement with education as a moral tradition.

Second, even if a procedural-liberal approach entails no authoritative commitment to any one particular ethical perspective (other than a commitment to the ideal of moral inquiry as an inclusive tradition itself) it does presuppose a basic interest and affective concern for the moral life on the part of those engaged in such moral deliberation. Anyone who seriously asks the question, "What ought I to do?" is already ensconced within and cares about a moral tradition – otherwise the question would be meaningless or perfunctory. The flip-side of this is that meaningful moral questions are at the same time pedagogical – they are asked within communities of practice that transform and change through the answering of those questions. The attempt to understand the moral life is by its nature pedagogical. Moral traditions can only come about because communities care to teach them and share in them with one another. When teacher candidates deliberate on the moral nature of their work with one another they exercise a commitment both to the value of what it is that they do and the moral life – by caring to explore its nature in the first place, and by teaching and learning with one another through the addressing of the question. Teaching and the moral life make common intellectual and motivation demands. Liberal education can work to ensure that teacher candidates experience these common demands together as opposed to compartmentalizing "professional ethics" and "teaching methods" as somehow disconnected.

FURTHER IMPLICATIONS FOR THE PURSUIT OF "RELEVANCE": PHILOSOPHY OF EDUCATION AND THE PUBLIC SPHERE

I have emphasized the importance of ensuring that the abstraction of philosophical ethics be tempered by a meaningful relationship with teacher practice in Faculties of Education. This is key to philosophical ethic's educational value, and so its relevance.

Much of what I have argued is framed within a debate partly internal to the politics of higher education and teacher education. But to see it as *entirely* internal would be misleading, for such politics extend into the public sphere. Here is why: So long as we already respect the value of teacher *education*, and not mere training, it makes sense to value a role for philosophy in education alongside other disciplines. But one can always ask why university-based teacher education is worthwhile to begin with, and why the public should fund it. In this case the value of philosophy for teacher preparation is questioned at a much broader, public level.

Philosophy is in a unique position here because to ask the question, "Is philosophy relevant?" is itself a philosophical question, for such a question asks for an account of knowledge and its contribution to living a good life and a good society. These are questions that only philosophy can answer. In other words, to ask philosophy to account for itself is to at the same time justify its relevance. So the transcendental argument I outlined earlier can be applied at this public level as well.

However, we can have good reasons for valuing X (transcendentally warranted or otherwise), but it does not follow that people will have the motivation or disposition to act on value X. We can offer good reasons for why, say, philosophical ethics is relevant and important for teacher candidates and why it should have pride of place within any cogent and morally responsible conception of professional formation. But the justification of the value of education for teachers is different from the political recognition of that value by the general public and by government. What I mean is that while we can be clear on the educational value of philosophical ethics for teachers, much hinges on the place of education within the larger society. As my opening comments suggested, this is a political question. As teacher autonomy decreases, so, too, the putative relevance of philosophy for teachers: Where teachers are not free to think and act the more indulgent the teaching of ethics, which presupposes a certain level of freedom to act, appears. Ought implies can, as the old saying goes.

The paradox of philosophy and political power is a very old one. Philosophers of education live and work in liberal democratic society where interests conflict, and a philosopher's interests in education are but one interest among many. There is no Platonic kallipolis for us to flee to. So when I think about "contested sites of education" for the philosophy of education, I'm often led to questions around the extent to which, and ways in which, philosophers of education should be engaging the political and public sphere. Public deliberation is necessary if our arguments about education are going to even marginally approach the kind of social impact they ideally should have if those arguments are as sound as we philosophers sometimes believe they are. The days of resting our case on the long history and intellectual authority of our home discipline are long past, if this ever was a viable option. Philosophers of education have begun to shift their scholarly attentions to government policy. Perhaps the next step would be to find ways to address the public directly (see Martin, 2011). When governments use the term *relevance* in the context of higher education policy, they presuppose a public who can make informed and educated decisions about what is relevance. The future of a higher education worth caring for largely rests on the redemption of such a presupposition. Philosophy of education can play a role in this redemption, or it can remain on the scholarly sidelines.

NOTE

1   A modified version of this chapter appeared in the journal *Curriculum Inquiry*, January 2013. Permission granted by *Curriculum Inquiry* with acknowledgment.

CHAPTER SEVEN

Developing Mindful Teacher Leader Identities in Higher Education

SABRE CHERKOWSKI

Increasingly, teacher leadership is recognized as an integral element of school reform and school improvement, with recent research suggesting that improving the professional capital in schools through developing the human, social, and professional capital of teachers is the key to transforming teaching in every school (Hargreaves & Fullan, 2012). For the past few decades, there has been a growing interest in researching teacher leadership to understand the different ways and means for teachers to engage as leaders in their classrooms and schools (York-Barr & Duke, 2004). This research is important to understand more fully how to encourage and support teachers in more diverse contexts and settings to take on leadership roles in the school as an opportunity to influence change and school improvement and to create more opportunities for continued personal professional growth in their work.

Teacher leadership is an emerging field of theory, with a clear definition not yet established. As a result, the concept can mean many different things to different people. For some, teacher leadership means taking on formal administrative roles in the school, while for others leading students in the classroom or leading colleagues to implement innovative curriculum and pedagogy defines what it means to be a teacher leader. The ethical and moral dimensions of teacher leadership have not yet garnered much attention, whereas the moral nature of formal leadership in schools has been the subject of significant research to understand the implications of applying an ethical lens to the roles and responsibilities of school administrators (Begley, 1999; Greenfield, 2004; Hodgkinson, 1991). In this chapter, I inquire into the implications of using a moral leadership perspective to think about teacher leadership. By doing so, I assume that teacher leadership can be broadly defined as leading learners for authentic learning. This definition is taken from educational ethicist Robert Starratt's writing (2004, 2005, 2007) on authentic learning, which he argues is a moral agenda that ought to be facilitated for all students by their teachers. Pursuing this moral agenda of authentic learning enables students to develop a truer sense of who they are, what they hope to become, and how their agency influences and is influenced by the relationships that make up our social and natural worlds. For schools, teaching for authentic learning necessitates a reconsideration of the purposes of education and a critical reflection on how we attend to developing a broader range of capacities for democratic responsibility and social justice. This democratic responsibility can be elicited as students and their teachers are empowered to engage in a collective journey toward intellectual autonomy, enabling them to notice constraints, barriers, and injustices of the traditional educational status quo and to engage, as active citizens, in the processes of social transformation (Walker, 2010). One of the aims of authentic learning is developing in each person, within the context of and in relationship to the larger community, a fuller humanity that empowers graduates who are more socially conscious and likely to influence society toward the end developments of human freedoms and justice (p. 481). This holistic understanding of education would include academic achievement but is not limited to and is not driven by the current pressures for high-stakes testing stemming from an accountability agenda for school reform driven by a corporate and market-based ideology (Ravitch, 2010).

With the growing awareness of the importance of developing professional learning cultures for school improvement (Hargreaves & Fullan, 2012; Kwakman, 2003; Stoll & Louis, 2007), framing teacher leadership as leadership for authentic learning provides a shift in perspective on the role of teacher educators as essential members of an interconnected system of learning in an educational landscape that spans early learning, through the elementary and secondary years, into university programs and beyond. When defined as a moral activity – as leadership for authentic learning – teacher leadership in higher education means more than taking on administrative roles and being an innovative teacher in the classroom. It means taking on the role of leading adult learners in authentic learning about themselves and their roles in the larger educational community. Within this context, I assumed that serving as a teacher leader of authentic learning is underscored by a broader belief about the moral nature of teaching as contributing to an engaged democracy, greater human freedoms and social justice, and personal development and achievement.

What are the implications of using ideas about authentic learning and educational leadership to view teacher leadership as a moral activity with the responsibility of engaging others in the moral act of learning? What are the challenges and opportunities of preparing teachers to be future teacher leaders who thoroughly understand, consciously apply, and intentionally use democracy, self-knowledge, cultural knowledge, habits of mind, and reflective learning and advocacy in their professional lives (Ball & Tyson, 2011 in Ragoonaden, 2013)? What does it mean to engage teacher educators as leaders of authentic learning within the context of their role in the university context? In this chapter I assume a moral perspective of teacher leadership using questions that are often asked about the moral nature of educational leadership in general – leadership for what ends, by what means, and for whom? I inquire into the challenges and opportunities at the university level in thinking about how to support and encourage teacher educators as teacher leaders of their students, teacher candidates. I begin with an overview of Starratt's (2004, 2007) arguments for educational leadership as a moral responsibility for engaging students in authentic learning and then provide a description of the current context and terrain of teacher leadership. I conclude with an inquiry into the possibility of developing the space for fostering teacher leadership for authentic learning in teacher education programs.

EDUCATIONAL LEADERSHIP AS A MORAL ENDEAVOR: LEADING AUTHENTIC LEARNING

Starting with the question of "leadership of what and for what?" (Starratt, 2007, p. 1) shifts the focus toward the moral nature of leadership. Leaders of a learning community are tasked with ensuring those under their care engage in learning. But what kind of learning is encouraged and supported? In his writing on the moral nature of leadership, Starratt (2007) argues for authentic learning as the goal toward which educational leadership should be striving:

> Authentic learning is a learning that enables learners to encounter the meanings embedded in the curriculum about the natural, social and cultural worlds they inhabit, and, at the same time, find themselves in and through those very encounters. That kind of authentic learning, I argue, is intrinsically ethical. (p. 167)

Authentic learning engages the student in her or his own personal moral agenda that is focused on how to "find, create, own, and be true to themselves" (Starratt, 2007, p. 168). This moral agenda is inherent to all humans. Learning is not an individual activity where knowledge is assumed to exist independent of the learner; it is a social and relational activity in which knowledge is constructed as individuals come to understand their relationship to all other aspects of the natural and social world. Knowledge is socially constructed and relationally understood. Schooling can be an opportunity for students, in community with other learners and their teachers, to attend to their personal learning agenda of coming to know themselves and the relationships that shape our social and natural worlds:

> It is not an agenda they can turn over to their parents, to their teachers, to the community elders, to the state. It is an agenda that tacitly unfolds for them every day of their lives, as they learn to negotiate relationships, neighborhoods, new challenges and unexpected surprises. It is an agenda that they do not shelve or surrender when they enter the school grounds; nor do educators have the right to demand that they do so. Moreover, this is not simply the agenda of isolated individuals. It is the moral agenda of their whole generation, the agenda of all the children in the classroom, the agenda not only of creating and fashioning "me" but the agenda of creating "us." Individuals have to find out how to belong as well as how to be. Being with and belonging contains specific moral challenges which help to define the "me" an individual is discovering how to be. (Starratt, 2007, p. 168)

Schools can serve as the learning communities for pursuing these agendas in a meaningful way, if we shift our thinking about the purpose and nature of schooling – away from the competitive pursuit of higher test scores toward a more holistic education that prepares all children to develop academic skills and talents but that also reflects a desire for uncovering and honoring a fuller range of skills, talents, dreams, and ambitions (Sahlberg, 2011). From a moral philosophy perspective, Nel Noddings (2003) outlines her arguments for educating for the attainment of personal and public happiness as opposed to the more narrow and constricted goal of economic success. She notes that there seems to be less and less debate about the aims of education and that our society has somehow decided that the purpose of schooling is to ensure individuals have access to financial opportunities that will contribute to growing a national economy (p. 4). She laments the acceptance of the economic purpose of education that leads to a narrow view of schooling where "students should do well on standardized tests, get into good colleges, obtain well paying jobs, and buy lots of things. Surely there is more to education than this. But what?" (p. 4). She argues that one of the aims of education could be to teach children how raise questions about what it means to be happy, in both the personal and the public domain, and to guide students toward developing a broad range of talents and skills that may lead to future happiness (beyond economic factors associated with paid work). She explains

> We do our students (and our society) a significant disservice when we define happiness entirely in terms of financial success. A good society will make sure that its people do not suffer from a lack of those resources that constitute objective happiness, but its educational system will encourage them to explore and appreciate a full range of possibilities for promoting happiness. Education, by its very nature, should help people to develop their best selves; to become people with pleasing talents, useful and satisfying occupations, self-understanding, sound character, a host of appreciations, and a commitment to continuous learning. A large part of our obligation as educators is to help students understand the wonders and complexities of happiness, to raise questions about it, and to explore promising possibilities responsibly. (p. 22)

Noddings argues that schools elevate academic skills and talent above practical skills and that, as a result, few children are adequately prepared for the lives that they might lead. As an example of the personal domain, she suggests that all children might not need high-level calculus skills, but that almost all will need capacities for parenting and keeping a happy home, and yet this kind of learning is rarely taken on in a serious way with most students. Similarly, few children will take the highly academic (and expensive) route to higher education, but all of them will become citizens needing to contribute to maintaining and improving their civil society, and yet schools do not attend seriously to providing ongoing and relevant learning about citizenship in our increasingly changing world. She cautions of favoring one set of skills, dispositions, or abilities over the other and argues instead for a balanced view of preparing children for the world in which they live now and in the future. Her argument for the aim of happiness at school and for life underscores the need for seeing the purpose of schooling beyond an economic outcome. While there may be debate about how to educate for happiness, and whether that should be the aim of education, I align with Noddings' assertions about the importance of questioning the aims of education, and I suggest that this critical reflection on the purposes and aims of education is important ongoing work for teachers and teacher educators.

Assuming a more holistic view of the purpose of education, schools would be the place to practice seeing, connecting, thinking, feeling, and acting in a variety of experiences meant to provoke responses to how students make sense of who they are and who they might like to become as they notice, understand, and then negotiate the various relationships that influence and make up their interconnected world. Teachers, as leaders of the authentic learning community, would work to provide learning opportunities for the students to work through their important personal moral agenda of learning, as part of what it means to engage with the subject matter in a community of learners. Leaders for authentic learning would recognize that

> the authenticity of the learner as a learner is at stake every day at school. The school either supports that authenticity or it warps and suppresses it through the routines of its pedagogy, through the very limited time, and space allotted for learning, and the hurried and harrying assessment procedures employed. If the work of learning implicates the personal authenticity of the human beings involved in it as well as the integrity of the subject being studied, then young people attending schools find themselves in triple jeopardy. They can find neither themselves, nor the authentic subject being studied, nor the integrity of the learning activity itself, in what they are made to do in school. (Starratt, 2007, p. 171)

Assuming that authentic learning is worth striving for at all levels of education, teachers as leaders of authentic learning communities are challenged with the moral responsibility of ensuring students have access to the kinds of experiences and opportunities that enable them to make important, deep, and meaningful connections to the subject matter in a way that constructs self-knowledge and make connections to experiences as they come to understand the public implications their actions may have within the safety of a caring and engaged community of fellow learners.

TEACHER LEADERSHIP: AN AWAKENING GIANT

For the most part, the role of the teacher has been understood as that of a leader of students in the classroom, shaping, planning, facilitating, and assessing the learning and development of the children they are charged to teach every year. That is not new. What is a relatively new idea is that teachers remain an untapped potential as leaders of other adults in their schools, districts, education systems, and larger communities and that this leadership can transform the teaching and learning of the other adults whom they influence (Lieberman & Miller, 2004). This idea of teacher leadership as an agent for school improvement is becoming an increasingly important area of educational research, policy, and practice. A common definition has not been determined, but York-Barr and Duke's (2004) description of teacher leadership emerging out of their meta-analysis of the research on teacher leadership provides a general description of the current understanding about teacher leadership. They describe teacher leadership as "the process by which teachers, individually or collectively, influence their colleagues, principals and other members of the school communities to improve teaching and learning practices with the aim of increased student learning and achievement" (p. 256).

Although the conceptualization of teacher leadership remains somewhat murky, with research happening from a variety of perspectives and frameworks and for a variety of intended outcomes, what is becoming increasingly clear is that teacher leadership is an untapped area of research and development and that, as Katzenmeyer and Moller (2009) suggest in *Awakening the Sleeping Giant*, this awakening holds promise and potential for improving education for all students. A growing body of recent research has affirmed that teacher leadership is a critical component of school improvement (Firestone & Martinez, 2007; Lieberman & Miller, 2004; Muijs & Harris, 2006), important for achieving the level of distributed leadership needed within schools for sustaining positive change (Fullan, 2006; Lambert, 2003; Slater, 2008), and one of the keys to transforming teaching in all schools (Hargreaves & Fullan, 2012).

As the demand for teacher leadership development increases in research and practice, university teacher preparation programs across the world are targeting teacher leadership as a particular program of study. Countries such as Singapore, Finland, and the United States have developed programs and streams of study within their teacher education programs aimed at developing the skills and attributes necessary for taking on the role of teacher leader at various levels of the education system (Campbell, Lieberman, & Yashkina, 2013; Goodwin, Low, & Tee, 2013; Hannele, 2013). The study of teacher leadership, as currently defined, tends to be explored in faculties of education, and in some private leadership centers, as sets of skills and aptitudes needed to carry out the leadership roles in schools, such as how to lead meetings, how to create and share a vision, how to coach and encourage professional development among colleagues, how to use data for decision-making, and other important skills and capacities. As Katzenmeyer and Moller (2009) point out, "while principals and other leaders are required to learn leadership skills, teachers rarely are engaged in building these skills" (p. 5). These skills are important and providing teacher leaders with these skills is a critical part of developing capacity for teachers to carry out administrative and more formal leadership roles in schools. However, coming back to the moral nature of leadership, if the intent is to lead authentic learning spaces where learners come to know themselves more deeply, come to understand who they are in relation to the natural and social worlds, and come to reflect on how they can contribute their strengths to the societies of which they are a part, then teacher leaders need further support to develop capacities for leading others in authentic learning. Leading authentic learning requires personal attention to the moral agenda of coming to know oneself more deeply and within the complexities of interconnected and diverse relationships and systems.

The research on teacher learning provides good insights for how to think about the role of teacher education programs in creating opportunities for developing the capacities and habits of mind for teacher leadership for authentic learning. Feiman-Nemser (2008) describes four broad themes of research on learning to teach as learning to know, think, feel, and act like a teacher. The first theme is a cognitive or intellectual conceptualization of professional learning characterized by the belief that teachers need deep knowledge of subject matter and how to teach it to diverse learners, of how children grow and learn, about curriculum and pedagogy, as well as classroom management and assessment among other dispositions, skills, and capacities (p. 699). Teacher-candidates also need to reflect on the moral and ethical responsibilities of teaching for authentic learning. Feiman-Nemser alludes to the moral responsibility of this theme with her emphasis on the importance of critical reflection as a key cognitive capacity and argues that "without an opportunity to examine critically their existing beliefs in light of new possibilities and understandings, teachers may ignore or distort new ideas and practices" (p. 698). This admonition for ensuring critical practice fits well with the notion of the moral responsibility of teacher leaders to reflect on their practice of guiding students in authentic learning. Without reflective practice, how will teacher leaders ensure they are attending to their students' authentic learning needs when these needs may or may not be reflected in the schooling demands coming from administrators, school districts, and ministries of education? Teacher leaders of authentic learning need to be reflecting on whose needs are being met (or not) in the classroom, in the school, and in the larger community.

Reflective practice is recognized as an essential tool for professional growth in schools and other organizational contexts. Intentional focus on reflection can create habits and dispositions for paying attention to the unfolding reality of leading authentic learning. This paying attention on purpose – mindfulness – can be an essential practice for teachers seeking to deepen their own learning about who they are, how they relate to others, and how they wish to contribute to shaping their world. This reflective disposition can also contribute to the development of teacher leadership as a professional identity. Research on professional identity for teachers identifies four assumptions or conceptions about identity – identity formation is influenced by social, cultural, and political forces; social identity is fluid and formed in relationships with others and is formed over time through constructing and reconstructing the meaning of stories over time (Rodgers & Scott, 2008, p. 733). The goal of authentic learning links well with this idea of developing professional identity over time – a striving toward a deeper understanding of who one is and what one can contribute to the interconnected and complex relationships that form our social and natural worlds.

HIGHER EDUCATION AS A SPACE FOR MINDFUL TEACHER LEADERSHIP DEVELOPMENT

Approaches to preparation that ask us to consider the ethical and relational dimensions and responsibilities of what it means to be a teacher leader are critical in these times of heightened school reform and rapid change. Who the leader is is central to what the leader does and requires a deeper understanding and awareness of one's self and how to negotiate the relationships that make up our increasingly interconnected world. Higher education has not necessarily been seen as the arena for a deeper understanding of self in relation to the social and natural worlds. However, Parker Palmer and Arthur Zajonc (2010) propose a new conceptualization of higher education that emphasizes the connection of the mind, heart, and spirit in learning. Their integrative model of higher education encourages a holistic learning environment in which students grapple with their identity as they gain knowledge and insight about their content area and think about their impact and influence on others. They argue that "higher education looses upon the world too many people who are master of external, objective reality, with the knowledge and skill to manipulate it, but who understand little or nothing about the inner drivers of their own behavior" (p. 49). Palmer and Zajonc argue that experiential and service learning opportunities are necessary for connecting students and their lives and experiences to the learning and the world of relationships of which we are all a part. This is parallel to Starratt's (2007) argument that learning for school-aged children needs to be connected to a relevant experiential learning opportunity that gives students a chance to make links between who they are, how they negotiate the interconnected relationships that make up their world, and how they see themselves as contributing citizens of that world. These experiential learning opportunities can happen at all levels of the education system and can offer the needed catalysts for shifting existing beliefs and ideas to open space for new ways of imagining the purpose of school, teaching, and learning.

A teacher education program based on notions of authentic learning would invite students, as teacher-candidates, to explore their sense of identity and grapple with questions about who they are, how they negotiate the many relationships in the school system, and their potential role to influence others as teacher leaders. This kind of learning can be provocative and can unglue long-held beliefs and assumptions. Students and professors would explore what it means to be a human (teacher) in a human-organized system (schools) and this can create disruptions, discomfort, and strong emotions as traditions and beliefs about schooling and education are disrupted, and sometimes discarded. Aside from the challenge of encouraging and supporting professors as teacher leaders for authentic learning, learning that is messy, noisy, unfamiliar, and unpredictable, how do teacher education programs support this kind of learning for teacher-candidates who look to gain employment in school districts that may encourage the educational status quo in their schools? This is a big challenge not readily researched in teacher education programs. On a small scale, I have experienced this kind of tension as a professor in a newly developed portion of a secondary teacher education program that aimed to develop authentic learning experiences for teacher-candidates.

Recently, a small group of professors worked together to construct and collaboratively teach a case-based, inquiry-oriented, integrated course that takes place over the summer as part of the Secondary Teacher Education Program offered by our Faculty of Education. As professors, we were challenged to reach outside of our individual teaching practice to work together to construct an integrated course combining three foundational courses in our education program. We planned for large-group sessions as well as regular meetings in smaller seminar groups that were more amenable to cultivating intimate learning communities where students would feel safe to go to the edge of their assumptions, and beyond, and interrogate many of their long-held beliefs about who they are and their taken-for-granted expectations about teaching and learning. In both the large- and small-group settings, we aimed to explore big questions such as: What is teaching, learning, schooling, and education and for whom and for what purposes? We designed experiential learning opportunities that had the students interacting with each other and discovering more about themselves and their ideas about schooling and education outside the normal confines of a classroom. In creating case-based learning opportunities for the students we reflected on our professional identities and inquired into our beliefs in relation to theory, practice, our own assumptions, and societal expectations. As a group, we negotiated how to provide course content, how to develop community with our students and each other as we collaboratively designed learning environments that elicited and encouraged us to bring our full selves to our work and to support and encourage students to do the same.

For me, the learning and teaching experiences of the summer session were profound. Many of the students shared with me that they were also deeply moved, shifted, and grateful for the shaking up of their long-held beliefs about what it means to teach and learn and for what purpose. However, as I wrestled with the tensions that accompanied shifting my own practice toward a more collaborative, student-centered, and inquiry-oriented pedagogy I noticed that I was raising questions for myself about what it means to disrupt traditional notions of education and schooling through teacher education and what it means to move out of our silos of expertise to integrate learning experiences for university students. As I engaged in conversation with my colleagues about these tensions, I was able to reflect on my values and beliefs. This experience gave me an opportunity to engage in authentic learning that had me inquiring into my professional identity and questioning my role in teaching, learning, education, and school for whom and for what purpose. I was reflecting individually and in my teaching group about my role as a teacher educator and my responsibility to students, communities, school systems, and our society.

This kind of reflective practice and deep questioning and thought is the kind of mindful teaching that can move us beyond our minds to connect to our hearts and spirits in our teaching and learning. Mindfulness is a concept that has recently been introduced to our faculty as part of what it could mean to be a teacher in our society. I am learning about the physical practices of mindfulness through learning about research on yoga, meditation, and self-regulation activities for students and teachers. I am thinking about what it means to carry out research on mindful educative practices and what it means to be mindful in my own teaching, research, and service commitments as I learn more about the science behind mindfulness that has been defined as "the awareness that emerges through paying attention on purpose,... to the unfolding of experience moment by moment" (Kabat-Zinn, 2003, p. 14). In writing about what it means to live a moral life, Maxine Greene (1978) wrote about the need for becoming wide awake as a necessary condition for exercising agency and that "only as they learn to make sense of what is happening, can they feel themselves to be autonomous" (p. 44). As a teacher educator, I am in the position of providing opportunities for my students to wake up to their past, present, and future experiences as teachers and to become intellectually autonomous, but only if I am fully awake to my beliefs, values, histories, desires, and experiences (Greene, 1978). This is a profound way of thinking about awakening to the power and potential of teacher leadership, and also a vulnerable space in which to dwell as an educator as I inquire into the choices that I might make about my teaching. Can I risk getting to know my students on a deeper level to enable me to personalize teaching content through activities, lessons, and assignments that take into account students' experiences and that highlight the public applications of this learning (Starratt, 2005)? Can I create community in my classes that invites others to awaken to the fullness of their human experience in schools? Can I open my practice to colleagues to engage in conversations about why I do what I do? Can I stay wide-awake enough to notice when I am pulled into the comfort of following paths toward efficiency, external measurement, and standardization? As with the challenges in schools for teacher leaders, the challenges in higher education are many for tenure-track professors who aim to serve as teacher leaders in this time of increasing accountability and pressure for measurable outcomes of our research and teaching. Understanding how to support this leading for authentic learning in these times of increasing financial and political accountability is an important area of research in university settings.

FINAL THOUGHTS: AWAKENING TO THE MORAL NATURE OF TEACHER LEADERSHIP

Teacher leadership is more than the sum of the parts of the skills that are needed to work in administrative and formal leadership roles in educational contexts. As has been described, teacher leadership can be understood as a moral endeavor that calls on cultural, emotional, and relational knowledge. Part of understanding what it means to become a teacher leader is recognizing and gaining awareness of the inner life that influences, motivates, responds, and reacts to the social fields (Scharmer, 2009) in which we operate as educators. Gaining a critical awareness of their own agency in the relationships that make up these social fields creates opportunities for teachers, and their students, to become aware of and able to enlist a broader set of capabilities that make up a fuller humanity and may empower them to contribute to processes of personal and collective social transformation.

Reflection, contemplation, rendering a thoughtful and informed account of one's own learning, and developing habits that enable teachers to participate in and lead professional conversations (ones that include both consensus and divergence of ideas) are skills and dispositions needed of teachers leaders for authentic learning. This shift in thinking toward the moral nature of teacher leadership in higher education, and in other school contexts, moves the responsibility of leading beyond formal administrative roles, peer coaching, or curriculum leadership toward engaging others in learning about themselves and their role in the larger community as a way of influencing a shift in educational landscapes – toward a broader aim of developing graduates with an awareness of their potential agency as engaged citizens, who seek to attain more than personal development and achievement by using their agency to contribute to greater human freedoms and social justice. Teacher education programs could become the space for engaging in the kind of authentic learning necessary for teacher candidates and teacher educators to awaken to this kind of teacher leadership.

CHAPTER EIGHT

Academic Identity Within Contested Spaces of a University in Transition

LYNN BOSETTI

The chapters in this collection reflect on the nature of academic work in the context of a new university struggling to determine its identity and niche within the higher education landscape in Canada. Shaped by historical and societal realities, identity, whether personal, professional, or institutional, is fluid and malleable, allowing us to make sense of who we are, the places we come from, and our relationships with others (James & Shadd, 2001). Individual and institutional, identity is in a continual process of construction and reconstruction, and the impact of negotiating this complex developmental process is a significant and, sometimes, traumatic experience (Dwyer, 1999; Mogadime, 2004). In a transition from a long history as a teaching university college to being a sister campus of a top research-intensive university, the complex dynamics of this process is reflected in the narratives and the scholastic initiatives of the authors. These colleagues recognize that with this affiliation comes a new identity, elevated expectations, a shift in the core mission, and dominant values that govern academic life, as well as policies and procedures designed for the established university. The core challenge for all members of this community, particularly former senior administrators and faculty members of the university college system, resides in stepping up to the uncompromising expectations to perform according to new professional and scholarly criteria, to interpret policies to address the regional context and capacity of a university in transition, and to provide the necessary support to instill confidence in faculty of their merit, potential, and success as a research university.

As the former dean of a Faculty of Education, I share in the concerns raised by the authors. As an administrator I was challenged by an array of moral and ethical dilemmas in providing academic leadership and strategic vision, support, and mentorship for faculty members at various stages in their career, while at the same time reconciling the aspirations and demands of senior administration whose focus is on bottom-line fiscal responsibility, student enrollment management, program rationalization, and institutional ranking. These economic imperatives, and instrumental measures for which deans are held to account, compel us to accommodate the neoliberal agenda in the defense of the continued viability of our faculties. The culture, dilemmas, and tensions expressed by the authors in this collection are symbolic of the sorts of constraints of academic leaders.

This transition phase from a teaching college to research institution creates the condition for some to experience the imposter syndrome: questioning whether they have the necessary qualifications or attributes to work in this elevated context. Despite their advanced degrees and professional recognition from colleagues and authorities, they are suspicious that their accomplishments are undeserved, chalking up their achievements to chance, charm, connections, and other external factors. They characterize themselves as imposters (Deaux, 1976; Young, 2011).

While the imposter syndrome seems indicative of the universal human condition, it is particularly relevant for those academics caught in this liminal space betwixt and between being university college instructors and their role and identity as university research professors. Since socialization into a research-intensive culture did not occur during their formative years, many of these mid- to late-career academics are understandably angst-ridden by the interior struggle of whether or not they are worthy of their role and status as a university professor. The impostor syndrome is not just about feeling out of place or unworthy – it is a symptom of a culture that falsely defines success and worthiness through the myth of meritocracy (Leonard, 2014).

Change is a human process that takes time to become part of the culture of an institution, faculty, and academic life. Institutions that were formerly colleges, then university colleges, and now research universities need time to establish procedures, policies, and organizational structures to support this new mission and grow into this new identity largely defined by complex rankings related to grants received from federal granting agencies and scholarly productivity based on a combination of publications and impact factors. Along with this transformative process, a shared vision of this bicultural focus on research-teaching environments needs to be developed and implemented. In this contemporary age, modern universities expect their faculty members to be not only capable researchers and active participants in academic life but also effective teachers (Daniel, 2008). Yet, many universities in Canada are re-visioning their mandate as research centers to include equitable recognition of teaching streams without providing important mechanisms to support this movement. Therefore, new faculty, attracted by the status of being research professors but hired into primarily teaching institutions, begin their careers in particularly vulnerable contexts. They come ready and eager to meet those research expectations but are burdened with program development at the undergraduate and graduate levels and consistently high teaching loads. The difficulty in a transition institution is that it takes time to build the culture and make sense of the expectations for this location, particularly in a stratified and competitive higher education system. Their niche has shifted up the ladder based on institutional affiliation, not necessarily merit. Faculty members do not have the benefit of experienced research professors to shepherd them through the process, nor the time as a community to articulate clear expectations regarding what is valued in terms of performance and academic work, yet expectations for tenure and promotion are determined by the established research university.

In our "transition" institution, we have leapfrogged some important developmental stages and are caught between the image and reputation of our established sister institution and our prior success as a university college. We are akin to the developmental stage of a toddler where we are clearer about who we don't want to be, or what we don't like, than who we are, and what we want to become. The established faculty members are those who weathered the transition, were grandfathered with tenure as associate professors, and maintain considerable influence through their service on academic standing committees and a strong voice in matters related to collegial governance and decisions. New, untenured faculty are eager to embrace the ethos of a research university but often marginalized or silenced by the dominant established faculty who have a vested interest in the status quo. This tension divides and fragments faculty members, creating silos that limit opportunity to coalesce around shared values regarding performance, research, teaching, academic life, and contest the oppressive demands for accountability.

The dynamics of university with these fractures among faculty and administration divert concentrated energy from calling into question the traditional pathway to tenure and the culture of academic life and opportunities to consider how to adapt criteria to reflect twenty-first-century realities based on innovation, creativity, and equity. By acknowledging that the transition from teaching-centered university colleges to research-intensive universities takes time, commitment, and energy, the community of academics must take seriously the responsibility for collegial governance and to interrogate the measures used to determine meritorious academic life.

Many of the stories, reflections, and experiences shared in these chapters will resonate with academics seeking tenure and promotion; however, their nuanced message is best understood against the backdrop of their particular context. Their experiences provide insight into the plight of the culture of ambiguity inherent in transition institutions indicating the need for mentorship in terms of valued work, seeking life balance, and addressing the longing for the freedom to engage in deep and meaningful work. Many of the authors allude to an inherent transformational potential in the moral and ethical imperative of our work as academics that provides the motivation to continue to pursue projects that take time, may not be valued because of their slower return in instrumental terms of productivity, but are deeply satisfying to our curiosity and intellectualism, and stand to make a significant contribution to our profession.

Kanpol (1998) raises the question, "To what end do we do what we do… to attain tenure and promotion?" The authors in this volume grapple with this question from various perspectives. Inherent in their explorations are tensions regarding the nature of academic life, what constitutes achievement, what is valued in the academy, and the desire for a richer, meaningful personal and professional academic life. We hear stories that demonstrate the willingness of young academics to perpetuate the relentless work ethic demanded by neoliberal ideology with little awareness of how this contributes to the culture of performativity and working conditions of their peers. Others reflect on the postmodern cynicism of hard-earned lessons by exploring personal narrative and reflection as a form of pedagogical examination and interrogation.

Marginalized sessional and adjunct instructors recount experiences of working endless hours teaching large numbers of students for little pay, while also attempting to maintain a viable professional work profile. Those in the professor of teaching stream are expected to undertake enormous teaching loads with little access to travel and research funds available to those in the traditional "academic" (research) stream, yet still expected to produce research related to teaching and learning and present at academic conferences. Along with these tales detailing the unforgiving work pace of teaching in the academy, there exists the realization that universities still reward research stars. Universities cultivate a roster of elite researchers, divesting them of obligations to teach or do service, and these research scientists can focus on scholarly output, preferably the sort of scholarship and research that can be commercialized. Their share of teaching and service is distributed among their colleagues, sessional instructors or doctoral students. Despite these inequities between teaching and research, novice academics are driven by the pursuit of tenure and with it the promise of job security and the opportunity to freely pursue their own ideas and interests.

The dramatic irony in academic life is that from the time we are graduate students, academics are socialized to believe we have the privilege of pursuing our soul work – a labor of love, offering innumerable non-material rewards. This serves as justification for low wages as doctoral students, 60-hour workweeks, and pursuing adjunct or sessional teaching with the belief it will enhance access and opportunity for a tenure-track position. There are few boundaries between academics' personal and professional lives because we are free to work anywhere, anytime. The committed professional, doing what he or she loves, is the hallmark of the self-managing successful academic with the freedom and responsibility to impose limits on himself or herself. As knowledge workers, we carry our intellectual capital, with the belief we maintain power and ownership over the means of production in the academy. Eventually, some of us come to realize this is a false utopia as the demands of performativity and the insecurity it engenders render thin boundaries between work and private, family time – our fragile identity fused to our professional status.

Professional faculties such as Faculties of Education are examples of faculties in this liminal space of scholar-practitioners, where the work of academics can be viewed as service oriented, their research often collaborative, applied, and field based, involving practicing teachers, garnering small research grants. Professors of education propagate their work in scholarly journals as well as those appealing to policymakers, school-based practitioners, and parents. In a sense they engage in a kind of vocational/professional training that is accredited by an external professional body. Education professors serve admirable social goals such as inculcating civic values, enhancing social mobility, and cultivating graduates with practical wisdom and ethical judgment to be productive members of a liberal democracy who take up meaningful lives.

Notwithstanding this meritorious work, faculties of education have historically endured the slights of marginalization at administrative and scholarly levels perpetuated by a tradition of disseminating accolades to faculties who research in the economically endowed areas such as health and sciences. The metrics of research-intensive universities used to assess research productivity, merit, tenure, and promotion, are not readily applied to professional faculties. At budget time, deans and department heads are called to defend the rigor and impact of the research and scholarly output of their faculty, and compete for their share of graduate student funding, many of whom remain working professionals and study part-time out of financial necessity. Deans are held to account for the success of their faculty in terms of scholarly productivity, teaching excellence, and developing programs that attract and retain bright students from both national and international contexts, to contribute to maintaining the high ranking of our institution in the higher education market, and to ensure we secure our share of institutional and government funding.

Transitions institutions are keen to demonstrate their merit in being included in the rank of research universities, and anxiously adopt corporate strategies to structure, manage, and reward performance to secure their place in an unfamiliar terrain. This aggressive drive to belong combined with an underlying insecurity of failing to be recognized as belonging, along with the fear of losing positional ranking, plays out in the culture of the institution, the motivation of senior leaders, and the subsequent demand on academic life.

CONCLUSION

As society moves into the progressive sphere created by twenty-first-century educational mandates, let us, in the prophetic words of the wise Gandhi, embody
the change that is needed to transform the culture of academia. As creative, self-
managing individuals we are responsible for imposing boundaries between our
professional and personal lives, for discerning what is of value in terms of what we
do and produce, and articulating what constitutes success for us.

Since our identity is so intimately fused with our work and what we produce,
it is difficult for us to say no to projects and research opportunities, or contracts
that might promise additional income and publications. We must rally against the
neoliberal ideology that has contributed to the cult of busyness in academic life.

Do we stay on the treadmill because we have lost perspective of what our life
and our work might be otherwise? Do we think this is what we are supposed to
do? Do we succumb to what we perceive as the required pace and level of productivity as dictated by market-driven forces? The chapters in this book speak
for themselves and have their own agenda. They are stories of alienation and dis-
illusionment with the academy and the desire to pursue research that is deeply
engaging, personally and professionally meaningful, and contributes to a higher
societal purpose, rather than instrumental means to ensure tenure and promotion,
thus feeding the neoliberal agenda of productivity.

Discovery, however, takes time, and sometimes decades elapse before the impact of our work becomes apparent. We cling to the belief that once we have tenure we will have freedom and time to pursue our interests; however, the pressure
for promotion keeps us focused on opportunities that will expand our CV and
annual reports. Perhaps unconsciously we have become instruments of the neoliberal agenda in our acknowledged achievement as academics. We have moved
through the ranks by demonstrating our success in terms of teaching excellence
and research productivity, perpetuating the demands of intellectual life and nar-
rowing the possibility for junior academics to choose an alternative pathway reflecting more work-life balance and the engagement in projects that require deep
engagement. It is clear that not every person who sets out to become an academic
has the disposition, motivation, and commitment to continue to pursue or be successful under the current conditions and expectations of academic life. Through
sharing our stories of our journey in negotiating the demands of academic life, and
the sorts of compromises we are willing to make in the process, we have a greater
awareness of how life might be otherwise, and how we might support one another
to challenge the existing conditions that constrain our lives, to get off the treadmill
and live more fully in the present.

Contributors

Lynn Bosetti, Ph.D., is a Professor of Educational Policy and Leadership Studies. Her research and teaching have focused on faith, identity and the common school, planning alternative futures for education, issues related to school choice, charter schools and more recently, university leadership in the new economy.

Catherine Broom, Ph.D., has more than 20 years of high school and university teaching experience in Canada and overseas. She has written on the history of modern schooling; postmodern theories and methods; critical thinking; social studies history, methods, and philosophies; and local and global citizenship.

Sabre Cherkowski, Ph.D., researches organizational well-being and flourishing in schools. Attending to strengths and positive outlooks, the results of her work have implications for how we think about the teaching and learning that goes on in schools and the benefits that may accrue from focusing on what works, what goes well, what brings vitality to people in schools.

Susan Crichton, Ph.D., has taught in rural and urban K-12 schools in British Columbia, California, and Australia. She was a faculty member at University of Calgary and is a visiting professor with Aga Khan University–Institute of Educational Development, Dar es Salaam, Tanzania and a Fellow of the Commonwealth Centre of Education, University of Cambridge. Her research interests include appropriate technologies, design thinking, design principles for challenging context, and the Maker Movement.

Christopher Martin, Ph.D., researches philosophy of education, moral and political philosophy. His current focus is on the moral, political and economic aims of higher education. He is the author of *Education in a Post-Metaphysical World: Rethinking Educational Policy and Practice through Jurgen Habermas' Discourse Morality* and *R.S. Peters* (with Stefaan Cuypers).

Karen Ragoonaden, Ph.D., publishes and researches in the area of the Scholarship of Teaching and Learning with a focus on Critical Pedagogy and Self-Study of Teacher and Teacher Education practices (S-STEP). As a qualified yoga instructor, the concept of Mindful Educational Practices is an integral component of her praxis.

Pamela Richardson, Ph.D., explores human development from critical and post-structural perspectives with a particular interest in giftedness and talent across the lifespan (Critical Ability Studies). Her works are infused by arts-based, poetic, interpretive and auto-ethnographic methodologies. Her diverse teaching areas focus on Special Education, Inclusive Education, Gifted Education, Adolescent Development, English Language Arts, and Teacher Inquiry.

References

INTRODUCTION

Appelbaum, D. (1995). *The stop*. Albany: State University of New York Press.

Ball, S. (2002). Performativity and fragmentation in post modern schooling. In J. Carter (Ed.), *Post modernity and the fragmentation of welfare* (pp. 187–203). New York: Routledge.

Ball, S. (2006). Performativities and fabrications in the education economy: Towards a performative society. In H. Lauder et al. (Eds), *Education globalization and social change* (pp. 692–701). Oxford: Oxford University Press.

Ball, A., & Tyson, C. (Eds). (2011). *Studying diversity in teacher education*. Lanham, MD: Rowman and Littlefield.

Bhabha, H. (1994). *The location of culture*. New York: Routledge.

Bradotti, R. (1994). *Nomadic subjects: Embodiment and sexual difference in contemporary feminist theory*. New York: Columbia University Press.

Christensen, C., & Eyring, H. (2011). *The innovative university: Changing the DNA of higher education from inside out*. San Francisco: Jossey-Bass.

Daniel, J. (2010). *Mega-schools, technology, and teachers: Achieving education for all*. New York: Routledge.

Emberley, P. C. (1996). *Zero tolerance: Hot button politics in Canada's universities*. Toronto: Penguin.

Hyde, L. (1979/2007). *The gift: Creativity and the artist in the modern world*. New York: Vintage.

Kanpol, B. (1999). *Critical pedagogy: An introduction* (2nd ed.). Westport, CT: Bergin & Garvey.

Kanpol, B. (2010). True to self and the institutionalization of a new public identity: It's NOT only up to Barack Obama! *scholarlypartnershipsedu, 5*(1), 23–30. Retrieved from http://opus.ipfw.edu/spe/vol5/iss1/3

Räsänen, K. (2008). Meaningful academic work as praxis in emergence. *Journal of Research Practice*, *4*(1), 1–19.

Shulman, L. (2005, Summer). Signature pedagogies in the professions. *Daedalus*, pp. 52–59.

Sullivan, W. M., & Rosin, M. (2008). *A new agenda for higher education: Shaping a life of the mind for practice.*San Francisco: Jossey-Bass.

Thomas, D., & Brown, J. (2011). *A new culture of learning: Cultivating the imagination for a world of constant change.* CreateSpace Independent Publishing Platform. Retrieved from https://www.createspace.com/

Trilling, B., & Fadel, C. (2009). *21st century skills: Learning for life in our times.* San Francisco: John Wiley & Sons.

CHAPTER 1

Apple, M. (2004). Race and the politics of educational reform. In M. Olssen (Ed.), *Culture and learning: Access and opportunity in the classroom* (pp. 299–314). Charlotte: Information Age Publishing.

Ball, A. (2009). Towards a theory of generative change in culturally and linguistically complex classrooms. *American Educational Research Journal*, *46*(1), 45–72.

Ball, A., & Tyson, C. (Eds). (2011). *Studying diversity in teacher education.* Lanham, MD: Rowman and Littlefield.

Barrón, N. (2008). Reflections from beneath the veil. Mainstream preservice teachers (dis)covering their cultural identities. In L. Bartolomé (Ed.), *Ideologies in education: Unmaking the trap of teacher neutrality* (pp. 181–205). New York: Peter Lang.

Bartolomé, L. (2004). Critical pedagogy and teacher education: Radicalizing prospective teachers. *Teacher Education Quarterly*, *31*(1), 97–122.

Bartolomé, L. (2008). *Ideologies in education: Unmaking the trap of teacher neutrality* (pp. 181–205). New York: Peter Lang.

Bascia, N. (1996). Making sense of the lives and work of racial minority immigrant teachers. In N. Bascia, D. Thiessen, & I. Goodson (Eds), *Making a difference about difference: The lives and careers of racial minority immigrant teachers* (pp. 1–14). Toronto, ON: Garamond.

Bourdieu, P. (1977). Cultural reproduction and social reproduction. In J. Karabel & A. Halsey (Eds), *Power and ideology in education* (pp. 487–511). New York: Oxford University Press.

Bourdieu, P. (1991). *Language and symbolic power.* Cambridge: Polity Press.

Brown, E. (2005). The (in)visibility of race in narrative constructions of the self. In J. Loughran & T. Russell (Eds), *Improving teacher education practice through self-study*. London: Routledge.

Casey, K. (1993). *I answer with my life: Life histories of women teachers working for social change.* New York: Routledge.

Côté, J. E., & Allahar, A. (2007). *Ivory tower blues: A university system in crisis.* Toronto, ON: University of Toronto Press.

Dewey, J. (1897). My pedagogic creed. *School Journal*, *54*,77–80.

Dewey, J. (1902). *The educational situation.* Chicago: University of Chicago Press.

Dewey, J. (1916). *Democracy and education.* New York: Free Press.

Dewey, J. (1927). *The public and its problems.* New York: Henry Holt.

Egbo, B. (2005). Critical pedagogy as transformative micro-level praxis. *AE-Extra*. Retrieved from www.unco.edu/ae-extra/2005/6/Art-4.html

Egbo, B. (2009) *Teaching for diversity in Canadian schools.* Toronto, ON: Pearson.

Emberley, P. C. (1996). *Zero tolerance: Hot button politics in Canada's universities.* Toronto: Penguin.

Gay, G. (2003). *Becoming multicultural educators: Personal journey toward professional agency.* San Francisco: Jossey-Bass.

Giroux, H. (1983). *Theories and resistance in education: A pedagogy for the opposition.* South Hadley: Bergin & Garvey.

Giroux, H. (1992). *Border crossings: Cultural workers and the politics of education.* New York: Routledge.

Grant, C., & Gibson, M. (2011). Diversity and teacher education: A historical perspective. In A. Ball & C. Tyson (Eds), *Studying diversity in teacher education* (pp. 19–61). Lanham, MD: Rowman and Littlefield.

Haberman, M., & Post, L. (1992). Does direct experience change education students' perceptions of low-income minority children? *Midwestern Educational Researcher, 5*(2), 29–31.

Heilman, E. (2003). Critical theory as a personal project: From early idealism to academic realism. *Educational Theory, 53*(3), 247–274.

Henry, A. (1995). Growing up black, female, and working class: A teacher's narrative. *Anthropology & Education Quarterly, 26*(3), 279–305.

Kanpol, B. (1999). *Critical pedagogy: An introduction* (2nd ed.).Westport, CT: Bergin & Garvey.

Kanpol, B. (2010). True to self and the institutionalization of a new public identity: It's NOT only up to Barack Obama! *scholarlypartnershipsedu, 5*(1), 23–30. Retrieved from http://opus.ipfw.edu/spe/vol5/iss1/3

Kanpol, B., & McLaren, P. (Eds). (1995). *Critical multiculturalism: Uncommon voices in a common struggle.* Westport, CT: Bergin & Garvey.

Kincheloe, J. (2005). *Critical pedagogy: A primer.* New York: Peter Lang.

Kozol, J. (1991). *Savage inequalities: Children in America's schools.* New York: Harper.

Laboskey, V. (2007). *The methodology of self-study and its theoretical underpinnings.* In J. Loughran et al. (Eds), *International handbook of self-study of teaching and teacher education practice* (pp. 817–869). New York: Springer.

Ladson-Billings, G. (2006). It's not the culture of poverty, it's the poverty of culture. The problem with teacher education. *Anthropology and Teacher Education Quarterly, 37*(2), 104–109.

McIntosh, P. (1989, July/August). White privilege: Unpacking the invisible knapsack. *Peace and Freedom,* 9–10; reproduced in *Independent School, 49* (1990), 31–35.

Mogadime, D. (2004). *Giving meaning to women teachers' life histories and political commitments in the class-room.* Retrieved from Proquest Digital Dissertations database. (Publication number AAT NQ78461)

Nieto, S. (2004). *Affirming diversity: The sociopolitical context of multicultural education.* Boston, MA: Allyn & Bacon.

Pajares, M. (1992). Teachers' beliefs and educational research: Cleaning up a messy construct. *Review of Educational Research (62)*3, 307–332 doi: 10.3102/00346543062003307

Palmer, P. (1997). *The courage to teach: Exploring the inner landscape of teacher's life.* San Francisco: Jossey-Bass.

Parhar, N., & Sensoy, Ö. (2011). Canadian teachers' conceptions of teaching. *Canadian Journal of Education, 34*(1), 189–218.

Peters, S., Alter, T., & Schwartzbach, N. (2010). *Transformation in higher education: Democracy and higher education: Traditions and stories of civic engagement.* East Lansing: Michigan State University Press. Retrieved from http://site.ebrary.com/lib/ubc/Doc?id=10514509&ppg=396

Pinnegar, S. (1998). Introduction to part II: Methodological perspectives. In M. L. Hamilton (Ed.), *Reconceptualizing teaching practice: Self-study in teacher education* (pp. 31–33). London: Falmer Press.

Preston, J. (2011). *Practices of aboriginal youth leadership: A multi world-view on the 21st century leadership*. Saskatoon, SK: Saskatoon Public School Division.

Samaras, A., Hicks, M., & Garvey Berger, J. (2007). Self-study through personal history. In J. Loughran et al. (Eds), *International handbook of self-study of teaching and teacher education practice* (pp. 817–869). New York: Springer.

Shariff, F. (2008). The liminality of culture: Second generation South Asian Canadian identity and the potential for postcolonial texts. *Journal of Teaching and Learning, 5*(2), 67–80.

Shor, I. (1992). *Empowering education: Critical teaching for social change*. Chicago: University of Chicago Press.

Sleeter, C. (2001). Preparing teaching for culturally diverse schools: Research and the overwhelming presence of whiteness. *Journal of Teacher Education, 52*(2), 94–106

Sullivan, W. M., & Rosin, M. (2008). *A new agenda for higher education: Shaping a life of the mind for practice*. San Francisco, CA: Jossey-Bass.

Villegas, A. M., & Lucas, T. (2002). Preparing culturally responsive teachers: Rethinking the curriculum. *Journal of Teacher Education, 53*(20), 20–32.

CHAPTER 2

Aoki, T. (2005). Layered voices of teaching: The uncannily correct and the elusively true. In W. Pinar & R. Irwin (Eds), *Curriculum in a new key: The collected works of Ted Aoki* (pp. 185–197). Mahwah, NJ: Lawrence Erlbaum.

Appelbaum, D. (1995). *The stop*. Albany: State University of New York Press.

Bai, H. (2005). What is inquiry? In W. Hare & J. Portelli (Eds), *Key questions for educators* (pp. 45– 47). Halifax, NS: Edphil Books.

Barone, T. (2008). How arts-based research can change minds. In M. Cahnmann-Taylor & R. Siegesmund (Eds), *Arts-based research in education: foundations for practice* (pp. 28–49). New York: Routledge.

Barone, T., & Eisner, E. W. (1997). Arts-based educational research. In R. M. Jaeger (Ed.), *Complementary methods for research in education* (2nd ed., pp. 73–98). Washington, DC: American Educational Research Association.

Bentz, V., & Shapiro, J. (1998). *Mindful inquiry in social research*. Thousand Oaks, CA: Sage Publications.

Boler, M. (1999). *Feeling power: Emotions and education*. New York: Routledge.

Chambers, C., Hasebe-Ludt, E., & Leggo, C. (2012). *Life writing and literary métissage as an ethos for our times*. New York: Peter Lang.

Dinnerstein, D. (1976). *The mermaid and the minotaur: Sexual arrangements and human malaise*. New York: Harper.

Eisner, E. W. (1981). On the differences between scientific and artistic approaches to qualitative research. *Educational Researcher, 10*(4), 5–9.

Eisner, E. W. (1991). *The enlightened eye: Qualitative inquiry and the enhancement of educational practice*. New York: Macmillan.

Eisner, E. W. (1993). Forms of understanding and the future of educational research. *Educational Researcher, 22*(7), 5–11.

Eisner, E. W. (1995). What artistically crafted research can help us to understand about schools. *Educational Theory, 45*(1), 1–6. Retrieved from http://www.wiley.com/bw/journal.asp?ref=0013-2004&site=1

Eisner, E. W. (1997). The promise and perils of alternative forms of data representation. *Educational Researcher, 26*(6), 4–11.

Eisner, E. W. (2005). *Reimagining schools. The selected works of Eliot W. Eisner.* New York: Routledge.

Fels, L., & Belliveau, G. (2008). *Exploring curriculum: Performative inquiry, role drama and learning.* Vancouver, BC: Pacific Education Press.

Foucault, M. (1973). *The birth of the clinic: An archeology of medical perception.* London: Tavistock.

Hirshfield, J. (1997). *Nine gates: Entering the mind of poetry.* New York: HarperCollins.

Hyde, L. (1979/2007). *The gift: Creativity and the artist in the modern world.* New York: Vintage.

Irwin, R. L. (2004). A/r/tography: A metynomic métissage. In R. L. Irwin & A. de Cosson (Eds), *A/r/tography: Rendering self through arts-based living inquiry* (pp. 27–38). Vancouver, BC: Pacific Educational Press.

Irwin, R. L., & Springgay, S. (2008). A/r/tography as practice-based research. In S. Springgay, R. L. Irwin, C. Leggo, & P. Gouzouasis (Eds), *Being with a/r/tography* (pp. xix–xxxiii). Rotterdam, The Netherlands: Sense.

Kenway, J., Bullen, E., Fahey, J., & Robb, S. (2006). *Haunting the knowledge economy.* New York: Routledge.

Knowles, G. J., & Cole, A. L. (Eds). (2008). *Handbook of the arts in qualitative research: Perspectives, methodologies, examples and issues.* Thousand Oaks, CA: Sage Publications.

Leggo, C. (2005). The heart of pedagogy: On poetic knowing and living. *Teachers and Teaching: Theory and Practice, 11*(5), 439–455.

Leggo, C. (2008). The ecology of personal and professional experience: A poet's view. In M. Cahnmann-Taylor & R. Siegesmund (Eds), *Arts-based research in education: Foundations for practice* (pp. 89–97). New York: Routledge.

Lorde, A. (1985). Poetry is not a luxury. In *Sister outsider: Essays and speeches* (p. 36). New York: Crossing Press. Retrieved from http://www.onbeing.org/program/words-shimmer/feature/poetry-not-luxury-audre-lorde/318

Lyotard, J.-F. (1993). *The libidinal economy* (Trans. I. Hamilton Grant). Bloomington, IN: Indiana University Press.

Marcuse, H. (1964). *One dimensional man.* Boston, MA: Beacon.

Meyer, K. (2010). Living inquiry: Me, my self, and other. *Journal of Curriculum Theorizing, 26*(1), 85–96.

Neilsen, L. (2008). Lyric inquiry. In A. L. Cole & G. J. Knowles (Eds), *Handbook of the arts in qualitative research: Perspectives, methodologies, examples and issues* (pp. 93–102). Thousand Oaks, CA: Sage Publications.

Stewart, K. (2005). Cultural poesis: The generativity of emergent things. In N. Denzin & Y. Lincoln (Eds), *The Sage handbook of qualitative inquiry* (pp. 1027–1042). Thousand Oaks, CA: Sage Publications.

Varela, F. (1987). Laying down a path in walking. In W. I. Thompson, (Ed.). *GAIA: A way of knowing – political implications of the new biology* (pp. 48–64). Hudson, NY: Lindisfarne.

Varela, F., Thompson, E., & Rosch, E. (1991). *The embodied mind: Cognitive science and human experience.* Cambridge, MA: MIT Press.

Verdonk, P. (2005). Painting, poetry, parallelism: Ekphrasis, stylistics and cognitive poetics. *Language and Literature, 14*, 231–244. doi:10.1177/0963947005054479

Willinsky, J. (1989). Getting personal and practical with personal practical knowledge. *Curriculum Inquiry, 79*(3), 247–264.

Wolgemuth, J. R., & Donohue, R. (2006). Toward an inquiry of discomfort: Guiding transformation in "emancipatory" narrative research. *Qualitative Inquiry, 12*, 1022–1139.

CHAPTER 3

Apple, M. (2006). Producing inequalities: Neo-liberalism, neo-conservatism, and the politics of educational reform. In H. Lauder et al. (Eds), *Education globalization and social change* (pp. 468–489). Oxford: Oxford University Press.

Bai, H., Bartley, H, & Broom, C. (2007). A dialogue on Foucault. *The SFU Educational Review*. Retrieved from http://journals.sfu.ca/sfuer/index.php/sfuer/index

Ball, S. (1999). *Global trends in educational reform and the struggle for the soul of the teacher!* Paper presented at the British Educational Research Association Annual Conference, University of Sussex at Brighton. Centre for Public Policy Research, King's College London. Retrieved from http://www.leeds.ac.uk/educol/documents/00001212.htm

Ball, S. (2002). Performativity and fragmentation in post modern schooling. In J. Carter (Ed.) *Post modernity and the fragmentation of welfare* (pp. 187–203). New York: Routledge.

Ball, S. (2003). The teacher's soul and the terrors of performativity. *Journal of Education Policy, 18*(2), 215–228.

Ball, S. (2006). Performativities and frabrications in the education economy: Towards a performative society. In H. Lauder et al. (Eds), *Education globalization and social change* (pp. 692–701). Oxford: Oxford University Press.

Broom, C. (2010). Conceptualizing and teaching citizenship as humanity. *Citizenship, Social and Economics Education: An International Journal, 9*(3), 147–155.

Churchill, L. (2006). Professor goodgrade. *The Chronicle of Higher Education, 52*(25), C1.

Duncan, G. (n.d.). Shifting discourses in higher education: The performance-based research fund in New Zealand. Retrieved from http://www.interdisciplinary.net/ati/education/tvk/tvk1/Duncan%20paper.pdf

Foucault, M. (2006). The means of correct training. In H. Lauder et al. (Eds), *Education globalization and social change* (pp. 124–137). Oxford: Oxford University Press.

Freire, P. (1998). *Pedagogy of Freedom: Ethics, Democracy, and Civic Courage.* Lanham, MD: Rowman & Littlefield.

Jayakumar, U., Howard, T., Allen, W., & Han, J. (2009). Racial privilege in the professoriate: An exploration of campus climate, retention, and satisfaction. *Journal of Higher Education, 80*(5), 538–563.

Glaser, B. (1992). Basics of grounded theory analysis. Mill Valley, CA: Sociology Press.

Johnson, H. (2005). Reflecting and talking about private lives and professional consequences. *International Journal of Children's Spirituality, 10*(1), 81–96.

Marshall, J. (1999). Performativity: Lyotard and Foucault through Searle and Austin. *Studies in Philosophy and Education, 18*(5), 309–317.

Martinez, K. (2008). Academic induction for teacher educators. *Asia-Pacific Journal of Teacher Education, 36*(1), 35–51.

Meng, J. (2009). Saving the teacher's soul: Exorcising the terrors of performativity. *London Review of Education, 7*(2), 159–167.

Murray, J. (2012). Performativity cultures and their effects on teacher educators' work. *Researchin Teacher Education, 2*(2), 19–23.

Palmer, P. (1998). *The courage to teach.* San Francisco: Jossey-Bass.

Polster, C. (2009). The privatization of higher education in Canada. In C. Levine-Rasky (Ed.), *Canadian perspectives on the sociology of education* (pp. 355–372). Oxford: Oxford University Press.

Strauss, A. (1987). *Qualitative analysis for social scientists.* Cambridge, England: Cambridge University Press.

University of British Columbia. (1960). *Faculty handbook.* Vancouver, BC: UBC.

University of British Columbia. (1962). *Faculty handbook.* Vancouver, BC: UBC.

Westheimer, J. (2003). Tenure denied: Anti-intellectualism and anti-unionism in the academy. In B. Johnson, P. Kavanagh, & K. Mattson (Eds), *Steal this university! The rise of the corporate university and an academic labor movement* (pp. 47–64). New York: Routledge, 2003.

Whittaker, E., & Ames, M. (2006). *Anthropology and sociology at the University of British Columbia from 1947 to the 1980s.* Retrieved from http://anth.ubc.ca/files/2013/03/ANSO-History-Whittaker_Ames_Ch.13.pdf

Wolfinger, N., Mason, M., & Goulden, M. (2008). Problems in the pipeline: Gender, marriage, and fertility in the ivory tower. *Journal of Higher Education, 79*(4), 388–405.

Youn, T., & Price, T. (2009). Learning from the experience of others: The evolution of faculty tenure and promotion rules in comprehensive institutions. *Journal of Higher Education, 80*(2), 204–237

CHAPTER 4

Agriteam Canada Consulting Ltd. (2013). *The People's Republic of China: Sichuan, Xinjiang and Ningxia provinces, strengthening capacity in basic education in Western China (CIDA): January 2001–September 2007.* Retrieved from http://www.agriteam.ca/projects/profile/strengthening-capacity-in-basic-education-in-western-china/

Bettis, P., & Mills, M. (2006). Liminality and the study of a changing academic landscape. In V. Anfara & N. Mertz, *Theoretical frameworks in qualitative research.* (pp. 59–72). Thousand Oaks, CA: Sage Publications.

Cameron, W. (1963). *Informal sociology: A casual introduction to sociological thinking.* New York: Random House.

Conteh, A. (2003). Culture and the transfer of technology. In B. Hazeltine & C. Bull (Eds), *Field guide to appropriate technology* (pp. 2–6). San Diego, CA: Academic Press.

Crichton, S. (2012). Using digital tools in qualitative research – Supporting integrity, simplicity, deep insight and social change. In C. Nunes Silva (Ed.), *Online research methods in urban and planning studies (pp. 284–298).* Hershey, PA: IGI Global.

Crichton, S. (2013, June). *Leapfrogging pedagogy: A design approach to transforming learning in challenging contexts.* Proceedings of the 8th International Conference on eLearning (ICEL 2012), The Cape Peninsula University of Technology Cape Town, South Africa.

Crichton, S. & Onguko, B. (2013). "Appropriate technologies for challenging contexts." In Stewart Marshall & W. Kinuthia (Eds). *On the move: Mobile learning for development* (pp. 25–42). Charlotte, NC: Information Age Publishing,

Daniel, J. (2010). *Mega-schools, technology, and teachers: Achieving education for all.* New York: Routledge.

Makoni, M., & MacGregor, K. (2013, December). Universities worldwide pay tribute to Nelson Mandela. Retrieved from http://www.universityworldnews.com/article.php?story=20131206121536315

Mandela, N. (2005, February). Speech given in Trafalgar Square, London, UK. Houghton, South Africa. Nelson Mandela Foundation. Retrieved from http://www.nelsonmandela.org/

Menand, L. (2011, June 6). Lie and learn: Why we have college. Retrieved from http://www.newyorker.com/arts/critics/atlarge/2011/06/06/110606crat_atlarge_menand?currentPage=1

Onguko, B. B. N. (2012). *Teachers' professional development in a challenging context – A study of actual practice in rural western Kenya* (Unpublished doctoral dissertation). University of Calgary, Calgary.

Räsänen, K. (2008). Meaningful academic work as praxis in emergence. *Journal of Research Practice*, *4*(1), 1–19.

Schumacher, E. (1973). *Small is beautiful: A study of economics as if people mattered.* New York: Harper & Row.

Shulman, L. (2005, Summer). Signature pedagogies in the professions. *Daedalus*, pp. 52–59.

Sousa, D., & Pilecki, T. (2013). *From STEM to STEAM: Using brain-compatible strategies to integrate the arts.* Thousand Oaks, CA: Corwin.

Spiro, M. (1990). On the strange and the familiar in recent anthropological thought. In J. Stigler, R. Schweder, & G. Herdt (Eds), *Cultural psychology: Essays on comparative human development* (pp. 46–61). New York: Cambridge University Press.

Stanford University Institute of Design. (2013). *Welcome to the virtual crash course in design thinking.* Retrieved from http://dschool.stanford.edu/dgift/

Thomas, D., & Brown, J. (2011). *A new culture of learning: Cultivating the imagination for a world of constant change.* CreateSpace Independent Publishing Platform, Retrieved from https://www.createspace.com/

Trilling, B., & Fadel, C. (2009). *21st century skills: Learning for life in our times.* San Francisco, CA: John Wiley & Sons.

TSL Education Ltd. (2012). *The world university rankings.* Retrieved from http://www.timeshigher-education.co.uk/world-university-rankings/2012–13/world-ranking

Turner, V. (1987). Betwixt and between: The liminal period in rites of passage. In L. Mahdi, S. Foster, & M. Little (Eds), *Betwixt & between: Patterns of masculine and feminine initiation* (pp. 36–52). Peru, IL: Open Course.

CHAPTER 5

Acker, S., & Dillabough, J. (2007). Women "learning to labour" in the "male emporium": Exploring gendered work in teacher education. *Gender and Education, 19*(3), 297–314.

Archer, L. (2008). The new neoliberal subjects? Young/er academics' constructions of professional identity. *Journal of Educational Policy, 23*(3), 265–285.

Armenti, C. (2004). Women faculty seeking tenure and parenthood: Lessons from previous generations. *Cambridge Journal of Education, 34*(1), 65–83.

Baldwin, C. (2005). *Storycatcher: Making sense of our lives through the power and practice of story.* Novato, CA: New World Library.

Belenky, M. F., McVicker Clinchy, B., Rule Goldberger, N., & Mattuck Tarule, J. (1986). *Women's ways of knowing: The development of self, voice, and mind.* New York: Basic Books.

Bettis, P., & Mills, M. (2006). Liminality and the study of the changing academic landscape. In V. A. Anfara & N. Mertz (Eds), *Theoretical frameworks in qualitative research* (pp. 59–72). Thousand Oaks, CA: Sage Publications.

Bettis, P., Mills, M., Williams, J., & Nolan, R. (2005). Faculty in a liminal landscape: A case study of college reorganization. *Journal of Leadership and Organizational Studies, 11*(3), 47–61.

Blackmore, J. (2002). Globalization and the restructuring of higher education for new knowledge economies: New dangers or old habits troubling gender equity work in universities? *Higher Education Quarterly, 56*(4), 419–442.

Bosetti, L., Kawalilak, C., & Patterson, P. (2008). Betwixt and between: Academic women in transition. *Canadian Journal of Higher Education, 38*(2), 95–115.

Bradotti, R. (1994). *Nomadic subjects: Embodiment and sexual difference in contemporary feminist theory.* New York: Columbia University Press.

Cixous, H. (1981, Autumn). Castration or decapitation? Trans. Annette Kuhn. *Signs 7*(1), 41–55.

Clandinin, D. J., & Connelly, F. M. (1994). Personal experience methods. In N. K. Denzin & Y. S. Lincoln (Eds), *Handbook of Qualitative Research* (pp. 413–427) Thousand Oaks, CA: Sage.

Clark, K. (2006). Degress of separation: An ourstory about working-class and poverty-class academic identity. *Qualitative Inquiry, 12*(6).

Connelly, F. M., & Clandinin, D. J. (1996). Teachers' professional knowledge landscapes: Teacher stories – stories of teachers – school stories – stories of school. *Educational Researcher, 25*(3), 24–30.

Connelly, F. M., & Clandinin, D. J. (1999). *Shaping a professional identity: Stories of educational practice.* New York: Teachers College Press.

Denker, K. J. (2009). Doing gender in the academy: The challenges for women in the academic organization. *Women and Language, 32*(1), 103–112.

Eisner, E. W., & Peshkin, A. (Eds). (1990). *Qualitative inquiry in education.* New York: Teachers College Press.

Ellis, C., & Bochner, A. P. (Eds). (1996). *Composing ethnography: Alternative forms of qualitative writing.* Walnut Creek, CA: AltaMira Press.

Gilbert, E. (2006). *Eat, pray, love: One woman's search for everything across Italy, India and Indonesia.* New York: Penguin Books.

Glesne, C. (1999). *Becoming qualitative researchers: An introduction* (2nd ed.). New York:

Heilbrun, C. (1988). *Writing a woman's life.* New York: Norton.

Heilbrun, C. (1999). *Women's lives: The view from the thresholds.* Toronto, ON: University of Toronto Press.

Hurlock, D., Barlow, C., Phelan, A., Myrick, F., Sawa, R., & Rogers, G. (2008). Falls the shadow and the light: Liminality and natality in social work education. *Teaching in Higher Education, 13*(3), 291–301.

Kraemer, L. (2011). From teacher's pet to dropout. *Globe and Mail*, May 18, 2011.

Lester, J. (2008). Performing gender in the workplace. *Community College Review, 35* (4), 277–305.

Luke, C., & Gore, J. (1992). *Feminist and critical pedagogy.* New York: Routledge. http://www.qualitative-research.net/fqs-texte/2–06/06–2-16-e.htm

Maguire, M. (2008). 'Fade to Grey': Older women, embodied claims and attributions in English university departments of education. *Women's Studies International Forum, 31*(6): 474–482.

Marso, L. (2006). *Feminist thinkers and the demands of femininity: The lives and work of intellectual women.* New York: Routledge.

Mason, M. A., Goulden, M., & Wolfinger, N. H. (2006). Babies matter: Pushing the gender equity revolution forward. In S. J. Bracken, J. K. Allen, & D. R. Dean (Eds), *Balancing act: Gendered perspectives in faculty roles and work lives* (pp. 9–29). Sterling, VA: Stylus.

Palmer, P. (2004). *A hidden wholeness: The journey toward an undivided life.* San Francisco: Jossey-Bass.

Pillay, V. (2009). Academic mothers finding rhyme and reason. *Gender and Education, 21*(5), 501–515.

Pitt, A., & Phelan, A. (2008). Paradoxes of autonomy in professional life. *Changing English, 15*(2),189–197.

Reimer, M. (2004). *Inside corporate U: Women in the academy speak out.* Toronto, ON: Sumach Press.

Richardson, L. (2000). *Writing: A method of inquiry.* Thousand Oaks, CA: Sage Publications.

Saunderson, W. (2002). Women, academia, and identity: Constructions of equal opportunities in the "new managerialism" – A case of lipstick on the gorilla? *Higher Education Quarterly, 56* (4), 376–406.

Turner, V. (1967). *The forest of symbols: Aspects of Ndembu ritual.* Ithaca, NY: Cornell University Press.

Turner, V. (1977). Variations of the theme of liminality. In S. F. Moore & B. G. Myerhoff (Eds), *Secular ritual* (pp. 36–52). Amsterdam: Van Gorcum.

Ward, K., & Wolf-Wendel, L. (2004). Academic motherhood: Managing complex roles in research universities. *Review of Higher Education, 27*(2), 233–257.

Wheatley, M. J. (2005). *Finding our way: Leadership for an uncertain time.* San Francisco: Berrett-Koehler.

CHAPTER 6

Beauchamp, T. L., & Childress, J. F. (1979). *Principles of biomedical ethics* (1st ed.). New York: Oxford University Press.

Bohman, J. (1996). *Public deliberation: Pluralism, complexity, democracy.* Cambridge: MIT Press.

Campbell, E. (1997). Connecting the ethics of teaching and moral education. *Journal of Teacher Education, 48*(4), 255–263.

Caplan, A. (1983). Ethical engineers need not apply: The state of applied ethics today. In S. Gorovitz et al. (Eds), *Moral problems in medicine* (2nd ed., pp. 38–43). Englewood Cliffs, NJ: Prentice-Hall.

de Ruyter, D., & Kole, J. J. (2010). Our teachers want to be the best: On the necessity of intra-professional reflection about moral ideals of teaching. *Teachers and Teaching: Theory and Practice, 16*(2), 207–218.

Floden, R. E. (1985). The role of rhetoric in changing teachers' beliefs. *Teaching and Teacher Education, 1,* 19–32.

Goodlad, J. I., Soder, R., & Sirotnik, A. (Eds). (1990). *The moral dimensions of teaching.* San Francisco: Jossey-Bass.

Griffiths, A. P., & Peters, R. S. (1962). The autonomy of prudence. *Mind, 71*(282), 161–180.

Habermas, J. (1990). *Moral consciousness and communicative action.* Cambridge, MA: MIT Press.

Hand, M. (2009). On the worthwhileness of theoretical activities. *Journal of Philosophy of Education, 43*(S1), 109–121.

Hansen, D. T. (1998). The moral is in the practice. *Teaching and Teacher Education, 14*(6), 643–655.

Haydon, G. (1986). Collective moral philosophy and education for pluralism. *Journal of Philosophy of Education, 20*(1), 97–106.

Haydon, G. (1999). *Values, virtues and violence: Education and the public understanding of morality.* Oxford: Blackwell.

Haydon, G. (2011). John Wilson and the place of morality in education. *Journal of Moral Education, 29*(3), 355–365.

Herman, B. (1996). *The practice of moral judgement.* Cambridge, MA: Harvard University Press. Higher Education Funding Council for England. (2009). Retrieved from http://www.hefce.ac.uk/research/ref/

Higher Education Funding Council for England. (2009). Retrieved December 30, 2009, from http://www.hefce.ac.uk/research/ref/.

Hirst, P. H. (1965). Liberal education and the nature of knowledge. *Philosophical Analysis and Education, 2,* 113–140.

Howe, K. (1986). A conceptual basis for ethics in teacher education. *Journal of Teacher Education, 37*(5), 5–12.

Huebner, D. (1996). Teaching as moral activity. *Journal of Teaching and Supervision, 11*(3), 267–275.

Kole, J. J. (2011). Teaching moral competence to pre-professionals. In D. de Ruyter & S. Miedema (Eds), *Moral education and development* (pp. 239–253). Rotterdam: Sense.

Kymlicka, W. (1993). Moral philosophy and public policy. *Bioethics, 7*(1), 1–26.

Louden, R. B. (1992). *Morality and moral theory: A reappraisal and reaffirmation.* Oxford: Oxford University Press.

Martin, C. (2009). R. S. Peters and Jurgen Habermas: Presuppositions of practical reason and educational justice. *Educational Theory, 59*(1), 1–15.

Martin, C. (2011). Philosophy of education in the public sphere: The case of "relevance." *Studies in Philosophy and Education, 30*(6), 615–629.

Oancea, A., & Bridges, D. (2009). Philosophy of education in the UK: The historical and contemporary tradition. *Oxford Review of Education, 35*(5), 553–568.

Peters, R. S. (1966). *Ethics and education.* London: Allen & Unwin.

Peters, R. S. (1973). *Authority, responsibility and education.* London: Allen and Unwin.

Pring, R. (2001). Education as a moral practice. *Journal of Moral Education, 30*(2), 101–112.

Pring, R. (2007). Reclaiming philosophy for educational research. *Educational Review, 59*(3), 315–330.

Putnam, H. (1983). *How not to solve ethical problems.* Lindley Lectures. Lawrence: University of Kansas.

Rawls, J. (2005). *Political liberalism.* New York: Columbia University Press.

Rehg, W. (2003). Discourse ethics. In E. Wyschogrod & G. P. McKenny (Eds), *The ethical* (pp. 83–100). Malden: Blackwell.

Sanger, M. N. (2008). What we need to prepare teachers for the moral nature of their work. *Journal of Curriculum Studies, 40*(2), 169–185.

Stengel, B., & Tom, A. (1995). Taking the moral nature of teaching seriously. *The Educational Forum, 59*(2), 154–163.

Stojanov K. (2009). Overcoming social pathologies in education: On the concept of respect in R. S. Peters and Axel Honneth. *Journal of Philosophy of Education, 43*(S1), 161–172.

Strike, K. A. (1999). Justice, caring and universality: In defense of moral pluralism. In M. Katz et al. (Eds), *Justice and caring: The search for common ground in education* (pp. 21–36). New York: Teachers College Press.

Strike, K. A. (1990). Teaching ethics to teachers: What the curriculum should be about. *Teaching and Teacher Education, 6*(1), 47–53.

Strike, K. A., & Soltis, J. F. (1985). *The ethics of teaching.* New York: Teachers College Press.

Strike, K. A., & Soltis, J. (2004). *The ethics of teaching* (4th ed.). New York: Teachers College Press.

Watras, J. (1986). Will teaching applied ethics improve schools of education? *Journal of Teacher Education, 37*(13), 13–16.

Weinert, F. E. (2001). Concept of competence: A conceptual clarification. In D. S. Rychen & L. H. Salganik (Eds), *Defining and selecting key competencies* (pp. 45–65). Seattle: Hogrefe and Huber.

White, J. (1973). *Towards a compulsory curriculum.* London: Routledge.

White, J. (1982). *The aims of education restated.* London: Routledge.

White, J. (2012). The role of policy in philosophy of education: An argument and an illustration. *Journal of Philosophy of Education, 46*(4), 503–515.

Wilson, J. (1979). *Preface to the philosophy of education.* London: Routledge.

Winch, C. (2012). For philosophy of education in teacher education. *Oxford Review of Education, 38*(3), 305–322.

CHAPTER 7

Ball, A., & Tyson, C. (Eds). (2011). *Studying diversity in teacher education.* Lanham, MD: Rowman and Littlefield.

Begley, P. T. (Ed.). (1999). *Values and educational leadership.* Albany, NY: State University of New York Press.

Campbell, C., Lieberman, A., & Yashkina, G. (2013). *Teacher learning and leadership in Ontario, Canada: Professional learning for high-quality and equitable education.* Paper presented at American Educational Research Association, San Francisco, CA, April 26–June 2.

Feiman-Nemser, S. (2008). Teacher learning: How do teachers learn to teach? In M. Cochran-Smith, S. Feiman-Nemser, D. J. McIntyre, & K. E. Demers (Eds), *Handbook of research on teacher education: Enduring questions in changing contexts* (pp. 697–705). New York: Routledge.

Firestone, W., & Martinez, M. (2007). Districts, teacher leaders, and distributed leadership: Changing instructional practice. *Leadership and Policy in Schools, 6*(1), 3–35.

Fullan, M. (2006). Leading professional learning. *School Administrator 10*(10), 63–70.

Goodwin, A., Low, E. L., & Tee, N. P. (2013). *Developing teacher leadership in Singapore: Multiple pathways for differentiated journeys.* Paper presented at American Educational Research Association, San Francisco, CA, April 26–June 2.

Greene, M. (1978). *Landscapes of learning.* New York: Teachers College Press.

Greenfield, W. D. (2004). Moral leadership in schools. *Journal of Educational Administration, 42*(2), 174–196.

Hannele, N. (2013). *Persistent work for equity and life-long learning in the Finnish educational system.* Paper presented at American Educational Research Association, San Francisco, CA, April 26–June 2.

Hargreaves, A., & Fullan, M. (2012). *Professional capital: Transforming teaching in every school.* New York: Teachers College Press.

Hodgkinson, C. (1991). *Educational leadership: The moral art.* Albany, NY: State University of New York Press.

Kabat-Zinn, J. (2003). Mindfulness-based interventions in context: Past, present, and future. *Clinical Psychology: Science and Practice, 10*(2), 144–156.

Katzenmeyer, M. H., & Moller, G. V. (2009). *Awakening the sleeping giant: Helping teachers to develop as leaders.* Thousand Oaks, CA: Corwin Press.

Kwakman, K. (2003). Factors affecting teachers' participation in professional learning activities. *Teaching and Teacher Education, 19,* 149–170.

Lambert, L. (2003). *Leadership capacity for lasting school improvement.* Alexandria, VA: Association for Supervision and Curriculum Development.

Lieberman, A., & Miller, L. (2004). *Teacher leadership.* San Francisco: Jossey-Bass.

Muijs, D., & Harris, A. (2006). Teacher led school improvement: Teacher leadership in the UK. *Teachers and Teacher Education, 22*(8), 961–972.

Noddings, N. (2003). *Happiness and education.* Cambridge, UK: Cambridge University Press.

Palmer, P., & Zajonc, A. (2010). *The heart of higher education: The call to renewal. Transforming the academy through collegial conversations.* San Francisco, CA: Jossey-Bass.

Ragoonaden, K. (2013). *Self-study and critical pedagogy: Setting the path towards emancipatory practices.* Paper presented at the American Association of Educational Research (AERA). San Francisco. April 27–May 2.

Ravitch, D. (2010). *The death and life of the great American school system: How testing and choice are undermining education.* New York: Basic Books.

Rodgers, C. R., & Scott, K. H. (2008). The development of the personal self and professional identity in learning to teach. In M. Cochran-Smith, S. Feiman-Nemser, D. J. McIntyre, & K. E. Demers (Eds), *Handbook of research on teacher education: Enduring questions in changing contexts* (pp. 732–755. New York: Routledge.

Sahlberg, P. (2011). *Finnish Lessons: What can the world learn from educational change in Finland?* New York: Teachers College Press.

Scharmer, O. (2009). *Theory U: Leading from the future as it emerges. The social technology of presencing.* San Francisco: Jossey-Bass.

Slater, L. (2008). Pathways to building leadership capacity. *Educational Management, Administration, and Leadership, 36*(1), 55–69.

Starratt, R. J. (2004). *Ethical leadership.* San Francisco, CA: Jossey-Bass.

Starratt, R. J. (2005). Cultivating the moral character of learning and teaching: A neglected dimension of educational leadership. *School Leadership and Management, 25*(4), 399–411.

Starratt, R. J. (2007). Leading a community of learners: Learning to be moral by engaging the morality of learning. *Educational Management Administration & Leadership, 35*(2), 165–183.

Stoll, L., & Louis, K. S. (2007). Professional learning communities: Elaborating new approaches. In L. Stoll & K. S. Louis (Eds), *Professional learning communities: Divergence, depth and dilemmas* (pp. 1–13). Berkshire, UK: Open University Press.

Walker, M. (2010). A human development and capabilities "prospective analysis" of global higher education policy. *Journal of Education Policy, 25*(4), 485–501.

York-Barr, J., & Duke, K. (2004). What do we know about teacher leadership? Findings from two decades of scholarship. *Review of Educational Research, 73*(4), 255–316.

CHAPTER 8

Daniel, C. (2008). *The educational attributes of some of the world's "top 50" universities.* Retrieved from http://www.uwa.edu.au/university/governance/executive/educationarchive/speech_on_world_class_universities

Deaux, D. (1976). Sex and the attribution process. In J. H. Harvey, W. J. Ickes, & R. F. Kidd (Eds), *New directions in attribution research* (Vol. 1, pp. 335–352). New York: Halsted Press Division, Wiley.

Dwyer, C. (1999). Veiled meanings: Young British Muslim women and the negotiation of difference. *Gender, Place and Culture, 6*(1), 5–26.

James, C., & Shadd, A. (Eds). (2001). *Talking about identity: Encounters in race, ethnicity, and language.* Toronto, ON: Between the Lines.

Kanpol, B. (1998). Identity politics: The dialectics of cynicism and joy and the movement to talking back and breaking bread. *Journal of Educational Thought, 32*(1), 57–74.

Leonard, D. (2014). Impostor syndrome: Academic identity under siege? *The Chronicle of Higher Education*. Retrieved from http://chronicle.com/blogs/conversation/2014/02/05/impostor-syndrome-academic-identity-under-siege/

Mogadime, D. (2004). Giving meaning to women teachers' life histories and political commitments in the classroom. Unpublished Thesis. Proquest Digital Dissertations database (publication AAT NQ78461).

Young, V. (2011). *The secret thoughts of successful women: Why capable people suffer from the impostor syndrome and how to thrive in spite of it*. New York: Random House.

Index

Barry Kanpol
General Editor

The Critical Education and Ethics series intends to systematically analyze the pitfalls of social structures such as race, class, and gender as they relate to educational issues. Books in the series contain theoretical work grounded in pragmatic, society-changing practices. The series places value on ethical responses, as prophetic commitments to change the conditions under which education takes place.

The series aims to (1) Further the ethical understanding linking broader social issues to education by exploring the environmental, health-related, and faith/spiritual responses to our educational times and policy, and (2) Ground these works in the everyday world of the classroom, viewing how schools are impacted by what critical researchers do. Both theoretically and practically, the series aims to identify itself as an agent for community change.

The Critical Education and Ethics series welcomes work from emerging scholars as well as those already established in the field.

For additional information about this series or for the submission of manuscripts, please contact Dr. Kanpol (Indiana University—Purdue University Fort Wayne) at kanpolb@ipfw.edu.

To order other books in this series, please contact our Customer Service Department:

> (800) 770-LANG (within the U.S.)
> (212) 647-7706 (outside the U.S.)
> (212) 647-7707 FAX

Or browse online by series at www.peterlang.com.